Soft and homey, with a crown of browned butter icing, these are best made with very ripe bananas. If you're a nut lover, add a handful or two of chopped, toasted walnuts to the dough after you add the dry ingredients.

spiced banana drops

1 cup (2 sticks) unsalted butter, at room temperature

2 cups packed dark brown sugar

4 eggs

2 cups mashed ripe bananas (about 4 bananas)

1 teaspoon pure vanilla extract

4 cups all-purpose flour

4 teaspoons baking powder

$^1/_2$ teaspoon baking soda

$1^1/_2$ teaspoons ground cinnamon

$^1/_2$ teaspoon salt

$^3/_4$ teaspoon ground cloves

Browned Butter Frosting (page 35)

In the bowl of an electric mixer set on medium speed, beat the butter with the brown sugar until fluffy. Beat in the eggs, banana, and vanilla. Sift together the flour, baking powder, baking soda, cinnamon, salt, and cloves. Add to the butter mixture and beat until blended. Refrigerate the dough for 30 minutes.

Preheat the oven to 375°F and line 2 baking sheets with parchment paper. Drop the dough from a tablespoon onto the prepared baking sheets. Bake for 10 minutes or until golden brown on the bottoms and just set. Remove to wire racks, using a spatula. When cool, frost with Browned Butter Frosting. Store in an airtight container for up to 3 days or freeze for up to 2 months.

MAKES 5 DOZEN COOKIES

Cookies
Year-Round

50 Recipes for Every Season and Celebration

Rosemary Black

PHOTOGRAPHS BY **Jonelle Weaver**

STEWART, TABORI & CHANG

NEW YORK

ALMOND BROWN SUGAR ROUNDS continued

Preheat the oven to 375°F. Remove the rolls from the refrigerator and unwrap them. With a sharp knife, cut each roll into 30 slices. Place 1 inch apart on ungreased baking sheets. Bake for 8 to 10 minutes, until the cookies are golden brown on the bottom. Remove from the oven and cool on the baking sheets for 2 minutes before transferring to a wire rack to cool completely. Store in an airtight container for up to 3 days or freeze for up to 2 months.

MAKES 5 DOZEN COOKIES

Published in 2007 by Stewart, Tabori & Chang
An imprint of Harry N. Abrams, Inc.

Library of Congress Cataloging-in-Publication Data
Black, Rosemary.
    Cookies year-round : 50 recipes for every season and celebration / Rosemary Black ;
    photographs by Jonelle Weaver.
        p. cm.
    ISBN-13: 978-1-58479-592-6
    ISBN-10: 1-58479-592-1
        1. Cookies. I. Title.
TX772.B5715 2007
641.8'654–dc22   2006022333

Editor **Dervla Kelly**
Designer **woolypear**
Production Managers **Jacquie Poirier and Devon Zahn**
Prop Stylist **Paige Hicks**
Photographer's Assistant **Tanya Guinsberg**

The text of this book was composed in Clarendon & Shag Mystery

Printed and bound in China

10 9 8 7 6 5 4 3 2 1

HNA
harry n. abrams, inc.
a subsidiary of La Martinière Groupe

115 West 18th Street
New York, NY 10011
www.hnabooks.com

This is a convenient dough to keep in the refrigerator at the holidays because you can slice and bake it into cookies at the last minute or whenever unexpected guests drop by. This dough also freezes well, so if you have extra time on the weekend, make a batch, wrap securely, and freeze for up to two months.

almond brown sugar rounds

$1/2$ cup unblanched almonds

$1/2$ cup (1 stick) unsalted butter, at room temperature

$1/2$ cup vegetable shortening

$1/2$ cup granulated sugar

$1/2$ cup packed light brown sugar

$1^{1}/4$ teaspoons ground cinnamon

$1/2$ teaspoon ground nutmeg

$1/4$ teaspoon ground cloves

$1/2$ teaspoon baking soda

1 egg

1 teaspoon pure vanilla extract

$2^{1}/4$ cups all-purpose flour

Preheat the oven to 375°F. Arrange the almonds on a baking sheet in a single layer and toast for 10 minutes or until they are colored. Remove the almonds from the oven and turn off the oven. Cool the almonds slightly, then process in a food processor until very finely chopped.

In the bowl of an electric mixer set on medium speed, beat the butter, shortening, and both sugars until creamy. Add the cinnamon, nutmeg, cloves, baking soda, egg, and vanilla and beat until combined. Beat in the flour. Stir in the chopped almonds.

Shape the dough into two 6- to 7-inch-long rolls. Refrigerate, wrapped in plastic, for at least 6 hours or preferably overnight.

continued

Contents

Tender little puffs that practically melt in your mouth, these are great to give as gifts or serve guests. A lavish coating of confectioners' sugar makes them look like mini snowballs.

walnut balls

1 cup (2 sticks) unsalted butter, at room temperature

$^1/_2$ cup confectioners' sugar plus more for rolling

2 cups all-purpose flour

$^1/_4$ teaspoon salt

$1^1/_2$ teaspoons pure vanilla extract

$^1/_2$ cup finely chopped walnuts

Preheat the oven to 375°F and line 2 baking sheets with parchment paper. In the bowl of an electric mixer set on medium speed, beat the butter until light. Gradually add $^1/_2$ cup confectioners' sugar and beat well. Add the flour, salt, vanilla, and nuts, and mix until well blended. The dough will be stiff.

Pinch off small pieces of the dough, roll into 1-inch balls, and place on the baking sheets. Bake 10 to 12 minutes, just until set. Don't allow the cookies to brown; they're done when golden on the bottom. Remove the cookies from the oven and place on a large platter. Roll in a generous amount of confectioners' sugar while still warm. Just before serving, roll in the confectioners' sugar again. Store in an airtight container for up to 3 days or freeze for up to 2 months.

MAKES 3 DOZEN BALLS

for my father,
Marcel Keith Black

Acknowledgments

Writing this book was the sweetest project I've ever undertaken because I love baking cookies, eating cookies and most of all, sharing cookies. Thanks to all my tasters, especially my husband, Steve, my children, Miranda, Molly, Karla, Kevin, Kerrie and Madeline, my father Marcel and my stepmother Huguette, and Regina Alvarez, Mila Andre, Cathy Andreycak, Shari Applebaum, Rosemary Carlough, Angie DeGaglia, Kristen Delancey, Cathy Elliott, Lisa Friedman, Norma Katz, Sanda Krasnansky, Carol Lampert, Pat Logan, Aaron Maine, Carla Manzi, Cathy Martyn, Steve O'Donnell, Bobby Ramden, Jamie Scios, Erich Sekel and Todd Soffian. And a heartfelt thanks to my agent Stacey Glick, my editor Dervla Kelly, designer Lana Lê, photographer Jonelle Weaver, prop stylist Paige Hicks, and food stylist Toni Brogan.

walnut balls

You can either use a cookie press and make small chocolate spritz trees or roll out the dough and use a tree-shaped cookie cutter. Either way, top with green sprinkles or frost with green icing and top with colored candies.

chocolate trees

$1^{1}/_{2}$ cups (3 sticks) unsalted butter, at room temperature

1 cup sugar

1 egg

2 teaspoons pure vanilla extract

$3^{1}/_{4}$ cups all-purpose flour

$^{1}/_{4}$ cup unsweetened cocoa powder

1 teaspoon baking powder

In the bowl of an electric mixer set on medium speed, beat the butter for 1 minute. Add the sugar and beat for 30 seconds. Add the egg and the vanilla and beat to combine. Sift together the flour, cocoa powder, and baking powder. Sift half the flour mixture into the butter mixture and beat well. Add the remaining flour mixture to the dough and beat to combine. The mixture will be stiff. Chill for an hour or so.

Preheat the oven to 375°F and line 2 baking sheets with parchment paper.

Roll out the dough to $^{1}/_{4}$-inch thickness and cut out tree-shaped cookies. Place on the prepared baking sheets and bake for 10 minutes or until set but not colored. Alternatively, fit the nozzle of a cookie press with the tree attachment. Fill the press with dough. Form cookies, leaving an inch of space between them, onto the prepared baking sheets. Sprinkle with green sprinkles. Bake for 8 minutes or until the cookies are set but not colored on the bottom. Remove the cookies from the oven and immediately transfer them to a wire rack to cool. Store in an airtight container, between layers of waxed paper, for up to 3 days or freeze for up to 2 months.

MAKES 5 TO 6 DOZEN TREES (DEPENDING ON IF YOU MAKE SPRITZ OR ROLLED COOKIES)

Introduction

There's nothing more sweet and satisfying to bake than cookies. When you feel stressed, bored, or just a little down in the dumps, the best therapy of all is to get out your measuring cups, turn on the oven, and get ready to immerse yourself in sifting, mixing, rolling, and shaping. Before you know it, the whole house smells wonderful, the kitchen truly seems like the heart of the home, and everyone in the family feels cherished and pampered.

Homemade cookies are beloved around the world for many reasons: they're special occasion fare and pretty. Cookies are finger food, meant to be held in our hands and savored as an energizing snack, a reward for a job well done, a dessert that can be childlike or sophisticated, and (okay—admit it!) even a breakfast on a rushed morning.

Preparing dinner day after day gets tedious, but cookie baking is always pleasurable and engrossing. It's the fun side of cooking, an activity to undertake when you just want to relax. As a family project, baking cookies yields sweet results, quality time together, and the tactile pleasures that all too often are left behind in childhood when we give up Play-Doh!

Few kitchen projects are as gratifying, with row upon row of handcrafted beauties waiting to be iced and dusted with sprinkles or perhaps cut into diamonds and drizzled with melted chocolate.

The word *cookie* comes from the Dutch *koekje*, which actually means "little cake." Persia was among the first countries to cultivate sugar, and many people believe that the first cake-like cookies were probably made in Persia in the seventeenth century.

CHERRY WHITE CHOCOLATE CHIPPERS continued

Drop the dough from a teaspoon onto the prepared baking sheets, leaving about 2 inches of space between the cookies, onto the prepared baking sheets. Bake for 6 to 8 minutes, rotating the pans top to bottom and back to front midway through, until the cookies are golden brown on the bottom and just set on the top. Watch carefully as it's easy to overbake these cookies without realizing it. Immediately transfer the cookies to a wire rack to cool completely. Store in an airtight container for up to 3 days or freeze for up to 2 months.

MAKES 4$^1/_2$ DOZEN CHIPPERS

1. **drop cookies**
   drop the dough from a spoon or finger onto the baking sheet

2. **bar cookies**
   bake the dough in a pan, then cut into bars

3. **icebox cookies**
   shape the dough into a log, refrigerate, then slice into rounds

4. **rolled cookies**
   roll out the dough and cut into pretty shapes before baking

5. **molded cookies**
   use a special mold or your hands to shape the dough into logs, balls,
   or another shape

6. **pressed or piped cookies**
   use a cookie press or a pastry bag to form the dough into various designs
   and shapes

Cookies range from homey to haute, from the simplest butter cookies to praline-topped caramel toffee squares. From holiday classics like candy-festooned gingerbread people to perennial favorites such as almond macaroons and black-and-whites, the collection offers something for the cookie lover in all of us. Need a serious chocolate fix? There are drops, squares, and spritz cookies laced not just with an abundant dose of chocolate, but with complementary flavors like mint, peanut butter, and even brandy. There are healthful cookies bursting with carrots, oatmeal, and nuts. Choose among soft, crisp, chewy, or spicy cookies.

Once you find your favorites, bake up extra batches to give as gifts, tokens of appreciation, or gestures of friendship. Sharing is all part of the cookie baking experience. With the offering of a tinful of homemade beauties or an invitation to sit down with a cup of tea and plate of fresh-from-the-oven cookies, invite your loved ones to taste the sweeter side of life. Bonding over a plate of cookies? It doesn't get much better than that!

These cookies offer contrasting flavors and colors: white from the chips, red from the cherries, and brown from the chocolate, and the sweetness of white chocolate offsets the tanginess of the fruit. Dried cherries are available in some supermarkets and most health food stores and gourmet shops, and they're great to keep on hand for tossing into salads and muffins as well. These cookies are ideal to pack and send as a gift at holiday time as they're not overly fragile, and they keep well.

cherry white chocolate chippers

1 cup (2 sticks) unsalted butter, at room temperature

1 cup sugar

$^{1}/_{4}$ cup light corn syrup

1 egg

1 teaspoon pure vanilla extract

$1^{3}/_{4}$ cups all-purpose flour

$^{3}/_{4}$ cup unsweetened cocoa powder

$^{1}/_{8}$ teaspoon salt

$1^{1}/_{2}$ cups white chocolate chips

1 cup dried cherries

Preheat the oven to 350°F and line 2 baking sheets with parchment paper.

In the bowl of an electric mixer set on medium speed, beat the butter with the sugar for 2 minutes. Add the corn syrup, egg, and vanilla and beat until fluffy. Sift together the flour, cocoa powder, and salt. Sift over the butter mixture and beat just until no streaks of flour are visible in the dough. Don't overbeat! Stir in the white chocolate chips and the cherries.

continued

cookie Family

Tools & Supplies

Cookie baking is both art and science—in precisely the proportions that you want it to be. You can go high-tech and surround yourself with pastry bags, presses, and molds, or you can get satisfying results with nothing more than a sifter, a handheld mixer, and set of measuring spoons.

One piece of equipment you'll definitely need is at least one baking sheet on which to position your unbaked cookies. Standard baking sheets measure 12 by 15 inches and have one raised edge, while jelly-roll pans (typically 10 by 15 inches) are about an inch deep and are ideal for bar cookies. Dark-colored pans will result in darker cookies after baking than those baked on shiny pans. Heavy nonstick pans are ideal for baking because the cookie bottoms won't burn. If you have a very thin baking sheet, simply place one pan on top of another to reduce the chance your cookies will burn. Other useful pans include an 8 by 8-inch square baking pan and a 9 by 13-inch oblong baking pan.

cherry white chocolate chippers

If you own a heavy-duty stand mixer such a Kitchen-Aid, you're a lucky baker indeed, as it can be used for everything from whipping egg whites to creaming butter. These freestanding mixers also mean free hands for you, since the beaters move in place and allow you to measure ingredients or wield a spatula with two hands. If you don't have the space or the budget for a big mixer, a small handheld electric mixer will get the job done, too. Performing nearly all the tasks a larger mixer can, it requires considerably less room to store.

For chopping nuts, making a variety of doughs, and pureeing fruit, it's hard to beat a food processor. A task that used to be painstakingly slow—chopping nuts in a manual grinder—can now be done in seconds in a food processor. (Once you invest in one, you'll use it for prepping ingredients for savory dishes, too.)

If you haven't already done so, invest in measuring spoons, dry measuring cups, liquid measuring cups, rubber spatulas in both a 6- and 9-inch size, and metal spatulas with 4- and 7-inch blades. The metal spatulas are helpful for removing cookies from the baking pans and for icing cookies, and you can also use them to efficiently scrape the last bit of chopped nuts or chocolate out of the bowl of a food processor.

A standard box grater is fine for most grating tasks, but you may want to get a citrus zester for when you need just a teaspoon or two of lemon or lime zest and you don't feel like picking it out of a box grater with the tip of a knife.

A rolling pin makes rolling out dough for fancy cookies so much easier. My personal preference is a wooden roller about 24 inches long, but there are also plastic and nylon ones. Have a couple of natural bristle brushes on hand for painting on glazes and egg washes. Try to buy brushes with black bristles since you'll immediately be able to spot a stray bristle on a cookie. Pick up some stainless steel racks so when your cookies emerge from the oven you have a convenient place for them to cool.

Parchment paper is a great invention and a real timesaver. Not only can you avoid greasing the baking sheets, but you can slide a full tray of baked cookies, parchment and all, right off the baking sheet and onto a cooling rack. Look for parchment paper at the supermarket near the waxed paper and foil; it is very inexpensive.

These are just about the richest, fudgiest chocolate bar cookies you'll ever taste, and the honey and corn syrup keep them extra moist.

double chocolate fudge bars

Nonstick cooking spray for the pan

1 cup (2 sticks) unsalted butter, at room temperature

2 cups sugar

1 cup unsweetened cocoa powder (preferably Ghirardelli brand)

$3/4$ cup light corn syrup

$1/4$ cup honey

$1^1/2$ teaspoons pure vanilla extract

4 eggs

2 cups all-purpose flour

2 cups (12 ounces) semisweet chocolate chips

Position an oven rack in the middle of the oven. Preheat the oven to 350°F. Spray a 9 by 13-inch baking pan with cooking spray, line it with foil, and spray the foil with cooking spray.

In a large mixing bowl, with the electric mixer set on medium speed, beat the butter and sugar together until light and creamy, about 2 minutes. Add the cocoa powder, corn syrup, honey, and vanilla and beat for 3 minutes on low speed. Add the eggs one at a time, beating on medium speed after each addition until the batter is smooth. Sift in the flour and beat until smooth. Stir in 1 cup of the chocolate chips.

Spoon and scrape the batter into the prepared baking pan. Bake for 40 to 45 minutes, until the center is just set. Watch carefully so the edges don't dry out. Remove from the oven and scatter the remaining 1 cup chips over the top. Return to the oven for 2 minutes. Cool the pan to room temperature. Refrigerate for several hours. Then turn out the panful of cookies onto a cutting board, peel off the foil, and cut into bars. Store, tightly wrapped, for up to 3 days at room temperature or freeze for up to 1 month.

MAKES 3 DOZEN BARS

Now for the fun part of cookie baking equipment: the cutters. It's advisable to have a collection for various holidays: stars, Santas, trees, and bells for Christmas; pumpkins and ghosts for Halloween; hearts for Valentine's Day; dreidls and menorahs for Hanukah; and eggs and bunnies for Easter. You can buy cookie cutters in many places, from mass retailers such as Target and Wal-Mart, to cookware shops. A variety of online sources are available as well. I prefer metal cutters to plastic as the cookies are easier to cut out and less likely to stick to the cutter.

Molds are needed to turn out fancy cookies called madeleines, a special treat that looks like an elongated scallop shell and tastes a little like sponge cake, but is crisp on the outside. Be sure to order the nonstick version of a madeleine pan and you'll save yourself the aggravation of scrubbing out the molds after you remove the cookies.

A cookie press (or cookie gun) has a decorative nozzle at one end and a plunger that forces dough through the tip to form cookies that look particularly impressive. You can buy a cookie press that comes with a whole set of tips, so you'll be able to produce stars, tree shapes, or loops in very little time. A cookie stamp, which is a ceramic or wooden cookie imprinter, allows you to flatten cookie dough and imprint a design into the surface at the same time. Gourmet stores and kitchenware shops are the best places to buy these.

For decorating with icing, chances are you won't need anything more than a small metal icing spatula. But if you enjoy indulging your artistic side in the kitchen by outlining cookies with piped-on icing or making fancy edging, you'll need to purchase a small pastry bag.

It's a science when you're measuring, sifting, and coaxing the ingredients to become a dough, and an art when you shade, frost, and decorate. But at all times, cookie baking is an engrossing and habit-forming activity that's fun to do solo or in a group!

 These cookies are great for young bakers to help with because the dough is rolled into little balls before being rolled in sugar. Be sure not to put the chocolate kisses onto the cookies until after baking, or the chocolate will scorch.

peanut butter chocolate kisses

$^1/_2$ cup (1 stick) unsalted butter

$^1/_2$ cup creamy peanut butter

$^1/_2$ cup granulated sugar

$^1/_2$ cup packed brown sugar

1 egg

1 teaspoon pure vanilla extract

$1^1/_4$ cups all-purpose flour

$^3/_4$ teaspoon baking soda

$^1/_4$ teaspoon salt

Granulated sugar for rolling

48 chocolate kisses (unwrapped)

Preheat the oven to 375°F. Line 2 baking sheets with parchment paper.

In the bowl of an electric mixer set on medium speed, beat the butter for 30 seconds. Add peanut butter and both sugars and beat until creamy. Beat in the egg and the vanilla.

Sift together the flour, baking soda, and salt. Sift the flour mixture into the butter mixture and beat until combined. With your hands, shape the dough into 48 small balls and roll each ball in the granulated sugar. Place the cookies 2 inches apart on the prepared baking sheets and bake for 8 to 10 minutes, or until the edges of the cookies begin to brown. Remove the cookies from the oven and immediately press a chocolate kiss in the center of each, pressing down so the cookie cracks around the edges. Cool for 1 minute on the baking sheets. With a spatula, remove the cookies to a rack to cool completely. Store in an airtight container for up to 3 days or freeze for up to 2 months.

MAKES 4 DOZEN COOKIES

peanut butter chocolate kisses

Understanding & Using Ingredients

Before you start baking, make sure you have everything you need on hand. There's nothing worse than getting halfway through a recipe only to discover you're out of a crucial ingredient! Here are the items to put on your shopping list.

SWEETENERS

Unless specified, recipes in this book call for granulated sugar. Brown sugar, which gets its color from molasses, is used in many cookie recipes. Whether or not to use light brown or dark brown is a matter of personal choice. Dark brown sugar simply has more molasses added to it than light brown. If you have only light brown sugar on hand, you can substitute it for dark brown sugar.

Confectioners' sugar is finely ground sugar that contains cornstarch to prevent clumping. An essential in many icings and glazes, it's sprinkled on top of some cookies for a decorative touch and is even an ingredient in some delicate cookies. Cookies made with confectioners' sugar tend to spread less because of the cornstarch in the sugar. When you sprinkle cookies with confectioners' sugar, always make sure your cookies are completely cooled first or else the sugar will dissolve.

Other sweeteners include honey; I like to use a light, delicate one such as clover or orange blossom. The more strongly flavored honeys, such as buckwheat, dandelion, or alfalfa, are delicious but tend to overpower the other ingredients in the cookie. An unopened jar of honey can be kept in the pantry for a year. If you refrigerate honey and it crystallizes, simply microwave it for about 30 to 45 seconds or until it's runny again.

When your recipe calls for molasses, which is made from the juice that's left when sugar crystals are extracted from sugar cane or sugar beets, you may use either light or dark. Light molasses, with a milder flavor and paler color, comes from the first boiling of the sugar syrup while thicker, less sweet dark molasses comes from the second boiling. Stronger-flavored still is blackstrap molasses, which comes from the third boiling.

The complementary flavors of butter and vanilla make these cookies a favorite. The dough is incredibly easy to make in a food processor, and uses only egg yolks—leaving you with just enough whites to make Pecan Meringues (page 78)! Sprinkle with colored or chocolate sprinkles, or leave plain.

classic butter cookies

1 cup (2 sticks) plus 1 tablespoon unsalted butter, chilled

1 $1/3$ cups all-purpose flour plus more for rolling

$1/8$ teaspoon salt

1 cup confectioners' sugar

3 egg yolks

1 teaspoon pure vanilla extract

Cut the butter into small pieces and place in the food processor, along with the flour, salt, and sugar. Process until crumbly. Beat the egg yolks in a small bowl and add them to the food processor, along with the vanilla. Process until it begins to form a ball. Wrap in plastic wrap and refrigerate for 10 minutes.

Preheat the oven to 350°F. Line 2 baking sheets with parchment paper. Flour a work surface and remove the dough from the refrigerator. Roll out the dough to a $1/2$-inch thickness. Cut out cookies using whatever 2- to 3-inch cookie cutters you like: round cutters and star-shaped cutters are especially cute. Place the cookies about 2 inches apart on the baking sheets. Reroll the dough and cut out more cookies. Sprinkle the tops with colored sprinkles or jimmies if you like.

Bake the cookies for 10 to 15 minutes, rotating the pans once during the baking, until the cookies are golden on the bottom. Remove the pans from the oven and remove the cookies to a wire rack to cool completely. Store in an airtight container for up to 5 days or freeze for up to 2 months.

MAKES 2$1/2$ DOZEN COOKIES

Molasses is labeled "sulphured" or "unsulphured," a term that refers to whether or not sulphuring was used in the processing. You won't find a substantial taste difference, although some people believe that the taste of unsulphured molasses is somewhat lighter. Feel free to use either in cookies.

Corn syrup, which is thick and sweet, comes in either light or dark. Try to use whichever one the recipe specifies, as there is some taste difference. Dark corn syrup is deeper in color and stronger in flavor. As a frosting ingredient, corn syrup lends flavor and body.

EGGS

All the recipes in this book call for large eggs. They should be well chilled if you plan to separate them, since it's much easier to separate a cold egg than a warm one. But eggs should be at or near room temperature when added to a dough or stiff batter. This is because adding cold eggs to a batter can cause the fat in the batter to harden, and this can change the final cookies. Of course, you wouldn't want to leave eggs sitting out on a countertop all day, but you can remove them from the refrigerator, along with the butter, an hour or so before you plan to make your dough. Another alternative is to place the eggs in a bowl of warm water and allow them to stand for 5 minutes.

If you plan to whip egg whites, they should be somewhere between chilled and room temperature because they whip best at around 60°F. One strategy is to separate eggs when they're cold, then allow the whites to sit for 10 or 15 minutes before whipping. If a recipe calls just for egg yolks, you may store the whites, tightly covered, in the refrigerator for three or four days. If the recipe calls just for whites, store the yolks in the refrigerator but be sure to use within two days.

FLOUR

Hard wheat flour makes excellent bread but not such fabulous cookies, which taste much better when made with a softer flour or a mixture of hard and soft flours. Most of the recipes in this book use all-purpose flour, which is a blend of high-gluten hard and low-gluten soft wheat flours. All-purpose flour is milled from the wheat kernel's inner part and does not contain the wheat kernel's germ (the part that sprouts) or the bran (the outer coating). Flour typically is enriched during the processing with nutrients like niacin, thiamine, and iron. All-purpose flour is interchangeable with unbleached all-purpose flour.

This easy-to-work-with dough makes a generous number of soft, spicy gingerbread men (or women), and after you frost them, the sky's the limit on decorations. Use your imagination, along with chocolate chips, raisins, small candies, or various colors of icing and sprinkles.

gingerbread men

1 cup packed dark brown sugar

1 cup molasses

1 cup (2 sticks) unsalted butter, at room temperature

2 eggs

5 cups all-purpose flour, plus more for rolling

3/4 teaspoon salt

2 teaspoons baking soda

5 teaspoons ground ginger

2 1/2 teaspoons ground cinnamon

1 teaspoon ground nutmeg

1/2 teaspoon ground cloves

Royal Icing (page 33)

In the bowl of an electric mixer set on medium speed, beat together the brown sugar, molasses, and butter for 2 minutes. Beat in the eggs one at a time.

In a large sifter, combine the flour, salt, baking soda, ginger, cinnamon, nutmeg, and cloves. Sift into the butter mixture and beat until no traces of flour are visible. Cover with plastic wrap and chill for at least 30 minutes.

Preheat the oven to 350°F and line 2 baking sheets with parchment paper. Dust a work surface with flour and roll out one-quarter of the dough to about 1/2-inch thickness. Cut out cookies using the cookie cutter of your choice. Repeat with remaining dough until it is all used. Bake the cookies for 5 to 8 minutes, until golden brown. Remove from the oven, cool for 2 minutes on the pan, and then remove to wire racks to finish cooling. Frost with the icing and decorate with sprinkles and assorted candies when thoroughly cool.

MAKES 5 TO 6 DOZEN GINGERBREAD MEN

Some cookie recipes call for cake flour, which is very finely ground flour that is bleached to make it white. It is a wonderful choice for many finer textured cookies. Whole wheat flour contains the wheat germ for more nutrients and fiber than white flour. Graham flour is whole wheat flour with a texture that is slightly coarse. All flours can be stored in the freezer for at least six months.

CHOCOLATE

While there's an incredible array of chocolates on the market today, you'll only need a few to make the recipes in this book.

Bittersweet, unsweetened (also called baking or bitter), semisweet, milk, and white chocolate are used in these recipes. To make milk chocolate, dry milk is added to the sweetened chocolate. In a pinch, bittersweet and semisweet chocolate are interchangeable, but because of the milk protein, milk chocolate should not be substituted for either one of these.

White chocolate, which is not true chocolate because it does not contain chocolate liquor, typically is made with sugar, milk solids, vanilla, lecithin, and cocoa butter. You'll also find a variety of chocolate chips in assorted shapes and flavors.

It almost goes without saying that the best way to choose a chocolate for baking is to taste lots of them and then make a decision based on your own personal preference! Since it makes a difference in the taste of the final product, chocolate is worth splurging on, so buy the best you can afford.

Another form of chocolate is cocoa, and you'll notice that it will be labeled either nonalkalized or alkalized (Dutch process). The difference is that alkalized cocoa is a little darker and less bitter. You can substitute one for the other in these cookie recipes.

When chocolate must be melted before adding it to the recipe, do so carefully. Either place the chocolate in a bowl and heat it in a microwave oven set on Medium, stirring every minute, or melt it in the top of a double boiler over barely simmering water. You can also melt chocolate with a fat, such as butter, before adding it to a recipe. Be sure to let melted chocolate cool before proceeding with the cookies.

gingerbread men

FATS

Unsalted butter is the fat of choice for most of the recipes in this book. Since it contains no salt at all, it is more perishable than salted butter. If you buy butter in bulk when it's on sale, you may freeze it for up to six months. Butter will keep, tightly wrapped, in the refrigerator for about a month. For these recipes, don't use whipped butter: it has air beaten into it and will change the consistency of a dough. For cookie baking purposes, also avoid the light and reduced-calorie butters, which have water, skim milk, and gelatin added to them. Try to stay away from using margarine and oil spreads, which don't have the same wonderful flavor as butter.

Butter causes a dough to spread more than vegetable shortening, so sometimes, when a slightly thicker but still butter-flavored cookie is desired, a half-and-half combination of butter and shortening is the perfect formula. It's best not to use all vegetable shortening since this can create a somewhat artificial taste. Avoid using vegetable oil as a substitute for melted butter since it alters the texture of the cookie. If you're watching your intake of saturated fat, it's better to have just one cookie made with butter than three made with vegetable oil!

LEAVENING AGENTS

Baking soda, or "bicarbonate of soda," is an alkali and it must be combined with an acid in order for a dough to rise. Common acid ingredients include yogurt, buttermilk, and even molasses. Since baking soda reacts as soon as it is moistened, doughs made with baking soda should be put into the oven immediately. Baking powder, which typically combines baking soda, cornstarch, and cream of tartar, comes as either double-acting or single-acting. In these recipes, use baking powder that says double-acting. Be sure to discard any containers that are more than a year old as they start to lose their potency.

FLAVORINGS

Concentrated flavorings pack a punch, so use very sparingly. Because they are so concentrated, only a very small amount is required. It's fun to try out a new flavor once in a while, too, so stock up on lemon, mint, and almond extracts as well as the one you'll use the most: vanilla. Extracts will last almost indefinitely. Always use pure extracts, not artificial ones, which have a chemical taste and can mean the difference between a so-so cookie and a great one.

These are the essence of what a good gingersnap ought to be. Ice them when cool with either the Basic Vanilla Butter Icing (page 33) or Cream Cheese Icing (page 34), or simply roll in granulated sugar before baking. Try these with pumpkin ice cream or pumpkin crème brûlée, or pack to give as gifts.

four spice gingersnaps

3 ¾ cups all-purpose flour

1½ teaspoons baking soda

1 tablespoon ground ginger

1 teaspoon ground cinnamon

¼ teaspoon ground cloves

¼ teaspoon ground allspice

¾ cup (1½ sticks) unsalted butter, at room temperature

2 cups sugar

2 eggs

½ cup molasses

2 teaspoons vinegar

Preheat the oven to 325°F. Line 2 baking sheets with parchment paper.

Sift together the flour, baking soda, ginger, cinnamon, cloves, and allspice.

In the bowl of an electric mixer set on medium speed, beat the butter with the sugar until creamy. Add the eggs one at a time, beating well after each addition. Add the molasses and vinegar and beat for 1 minute on medium speed. Sift in the flour mixture and beat until no flour streaks remain in the dough.

Form into 1-inch balls and place on the prepared baking sheets about 2 inches apart. Bake for 10 to 15 minutes or until the tops are crinkled and the bottoms are golden. Cool for 1 minute on the baking sheets, then remove to a rack to finish cooling. Store in an airtight container for up to 3 days or freeze for up to 2 months.

MAKES 8 DOZEN GINGERSNAPS

Both nuts and dried fruits add texture and flavor to cookies, and if you don't like one variety you can often substitute another. Toasting nuts before putting them into a dough or batter intensifies their flavor. Nuts can be frozen successfully for months, and you can chop them in a food processor while they are still frozen— no need to thaw. When chopping nuts, pulse them a few times and then take a peek. You don't want to overprocess nuts or you'll end up with nut butter rather than chopped nuts.

Don't forget about using whole nuts on top of cookies. If you frost an almond cookie, for instance, top it with a whole blanched almond or with some slivered toasted almonds.

When buying raisins, buy organic if possible as they taste much better. Both dark and golden raisins as well as currants can be plumped up by bringing them to a boil in a small pan, covered with water. Once they boil, remove from heat, set aside for 10 minutes, then drain and use. Instead of water, you also can "marinate" dried fruits in orange juice or even in rum.

Winter

Meanwhile, in the bowl of an electric mixer set on medium speed, beat the eggs until foamy. Beat in the granulated sugar and vanilla. Sift together the flour, baking powder, and salt and sift into the egg mixture. Beat briefly. Add the cooled chocolate mixture and beat to combine. Scrape the mixture into the prepared pan and press evenly out to the sides. Bake for 20 to 25 minutes, watching carefully so the bars don't overbake. It's okay if they are slightly jiggly in the center.

To make the mint cream layer:
Warm the milk just slightly in a small saucepan or in the microwave. Beat in the butter, confectioners' sugar, and peppermint extract.

To make the glaze:
In a small saucepan, stir together the chips, butter, and milk. Cook over low heat until the chips are melted, stirring constantly. Remove from the heat and add the confectioners' sugar. Beat or stir vigorously until smooth. If not thin enough to pour, add 1 to 2 tablespoons of milk.

When the brownies are slightly cool, spread the mint layer over the top of the brownies. Drizzle the glaze over the mint layer. Allow to cool for about 1 hour and then cut into bars. Store in a single layer in the refrigerator for up to 3 days. These cookies do not freeze well.

MAKES 3 DOZEN SQUARES

Cookie Science: how to mix, shape & bake the best cookies ever

Making cookies is a very personal experience and one batch never seems to turn out quite like another, even when you follow the exact recipe twice. Ovens heat differently and have "hot spots," cooks handle ingredients in different ways, and even the ingredients themselves can differ in brand or temperature from one recipe to the next. For instance, using a room temperature rather than a cold egg can affect the final cookie. So can adding skim rather than whole milk, or sifting versus not sifting the flour. Here's a little guidance on how to measure, mix, shape, and bake the dough so that the finished cookies not only look picture perfect, they taste so good you'll be making a double batch next time!

TYPES OF COOKIES

All cookies fall into several categories. The most common (and easy) are **drop cookies**, including old favorites like chocolate chip, oatmeal, and sugar. These are typically mixed in one bowl and then dropped from a spoon right onto the baking sheets. **Rolled, shaped, or molded** cookies are usually chilled for easier handling. Then they are either rolled out on a floured board and cut into shapes, shaped into a log and cut into rounds, or pressed into a special mold. Rolled and shaped cookies rely on a fairly stiff dough. It's important to resist adding too much flour to these, though, since an excess of flour can make for dry, rather than crisp cookies.

Bar cookies, including lemon bars, brownies, streusel-topped fruit squares, and granola bars, are very easy to assemble and a good choice for the time-pressed baker.

Piped or pressed cookies such as spritz are more fragile and time-consuming than the other categories. Though the dough for piped cookies isn't as forgiving as the dough for a drop cookie, these can be impressive to look at and fabulous to eat. From the Latin *bis coctum* (twice baked), biscotti are very crisp and come in

19

A layer of mint cream and a buttery chocolate glaze crown these fudgy bars, which may be cut into squares or diamonds. If you store them in the refrigerator, the mint flavor intensifies. This is a nice cookie to make for a school bake sale or an autumn party.

chocolate mint squares

Butter for the baking pan

For the brownie layer:

$^2/_3$	cup unsalted butter
Three	1-ounce squares unsweetened chocolate
2	eggs
2	cups granulated sugar
$1^1/_2$	teaspoons pure vanilla extract
$1^1/_2$	cups all-purpose flour
1	teaspoon baking powder
$^1/_8$	teaspoon salt

For the mint cream layer:

3	tablespoons milk
3	tablespoons unsalted butter, at room temperature
$1^1/_4$	cups confectioners' sugar
$^1/_4$	teaspoon peppermint extract

For the glaze:

$1^1/_2$	cups (9 ounces) semisweet chocolate chips
3	tablespoons unsalted butter
6	tablespoons milk
$1^1/_2$	cups confectioners' sugar

Preheat the oven to 350°F. Lightly butter a 9 by 13-inch baking pan.

To make the brownie:
Melt the butter and the chocolate together in the microwave on medium speed at 1 minute increments, stirring after each minute. When melted, remove from the microwave and cool slightly.

continued

all manner of varieties—even chocolate chip and fruit biscotti. The logs of dough are flattened, baked, and then sliced crosswise. A second baking results in a dry, crisp cookie that elevates a cup of espresso or cappuccino to a special treat.

MEASURING & MIXING

Use a glass measure, which has a pour spout and calibrated markings on the side for liquid ingredients, and a measuring cup with a flat rim for dry ingredients. This lets you level off flour and sugar with a straight edge and ensures that you don't add too much to a dough, which can completely change the texture of the finished product. To measure flour, stir it up a little in the canister, then scoop it into your measuring cup and press it down slightly to level. Make sure to level off a cup of sugar, too, and pack brown sugar firmly into a cup.

When you measure a liquid sweetener such as honey, corn syrup, or molasses, spray the cup with a little nonstick cooking spray first and the cup will be much easier to wash.

Try to have your ingredients at room temperature before getting started, and keep a sifter handy. This way you can simply measure the dry ingredients right into the sifter and they'll be ready to add to the dough.

Most cookie doughs call for you to beat the fat with the sweetener and then add the eggs and flavorings. Don't overbeat or the cookies can be hard and tough.

SHAPING & BAKING

For drop cookies, using two spoons means you don't have to get your hands covered with dough. Simply scoop a dollop of dough onto one spoon and push it off with another. If the scoop or spoon starts to stick to the dough, rinse it off in cold water and wipe off any bits of dough. Drop cookies are easy to make but be sure the cookies are all about the same size so they will bake evenly. These cookies tend to spread and flatten, so leave about 2 inches of space between each one. Since the dough can spread out too fast on a hot baking sheet, let the baking sheets cool a little when they emerge from the oven. If you need to use it again right away because you don't have extra baking sheets, wait 5 minutes and then cool off the baking sheet by running it briefly under cold water.

Who says pizza has to be made with cheese and tomato sauce? This dessert version may turn out to be your favorite pie of all because it's colorful, crunchy, and great for a party. By the way, the best tool for cutting this pie is—you guessed it—a pizza cutter!

chocolate chip candy pizza

1 cup all-purpose flour

$1/2$ teaspoon baking soda

$1/4$ teaspoon salt

6 tablespoons ($3/4$ stick) unsalted butter, melted and cooled

$2/3$ cup packed light brown sugar

$1^1/2$ teaspoons pure vanilla extract

1 egg

1 cup milk chocolate chips

$1/2$ cup chopped pecans

1 cup colorful chocolate coated candies, such as M & M's

Colored sprinkles of your choice (optional)

Preheat the oven to 375°F and line a baking sheet with parchment paper. Sift together the flour, baking soda, and salt.

In the bowl of an electric mixer set on medium speed, beat the melted butter with the brown sugar, vanilla, and egg until well blended. Add the flour mixture and beat just until combined. Stir in the chips and the pecans.

Scrape the dough onto the baking sheet and flatten into an 8-inch round. Pressing a piece of waxed paper over the top will help smooth it out. The edges should be as even as possible. Bake for 10 minutes. Remove from oven. Sprinkle the top of the pie with the chocolate-coated candies and with sprinkles. Bake for 10 more minutes, until the "pizza" is golden brown. Cool for 5 minutes on the baking sheet. Remove to a large plate and slice into wedges. Store, tightly wrapped, at room temperature for up to 3 days or freeze for up to 1 month.

MAKES 10 WEDGES

When you are shaping slice-and-bake cookies or biscotti, resist the urge to add extra flour. If the dough is really sticky, refrigerate it for 30 minutes or so and chances are that it will firm right up and you'll be able to handle it with ease.

Rolling cookie dough into little balls is the first step to making some cookies like Iced Lemon Snowdrops or Walnut Balls. For a little extra crunch and flavor, roll the cookies in granulated sugar or a mixture of sugar and cinnamon before baking. Some rolled cookies—like Double Peanut Butter Cookies—are flattened in a crisscross pattern before being popped into the oven. Whenever the fork sticks in the dough, moisten with a little water and continue.

Slice-and-bake cookies are easy to form if you shape them into a log, then place on a length of waxed paper and roll and smooth it in the paper. For forming the log for biscotti, try dropping the dough by the spoonful onto the baking sheet. Then you can shape and mold it into a log right on the baking sheet.

Shortbread offers you a couple of different options. You can bake it in a pan and then cut it into fingers afterward, or you may buy a special shortbread mold and bake the cookies in this. These come out looking quite fancy and authentically Scottish, and you can just cut them into wedges.

When you make pressed and piped cookies, it's important that the dough is firm enough so it doesn't crumble when it is extruded through the plates of the cookie press, yet it shouldn't be so soft that it doesn't hold its shape on the baking pan. It's a good idea to do a "test run" by baking one panful of cookies and then assessing whether the dough is the right consistency or not.

Cutout cookies require that you start with chilled dough. Dust the ball of dough with a little flour or confectioners' sugar and let it sit at room temperature for about 10 minutes. Place the dough on a clean, very lightly floured work surface and use a rolling pin to gently but firmly roll out the dough into a circle. If you want a sturdy cookie, like a gingerbread man, the dough should be a little thicker, up to about $1/4$ inch. When the dough is about $1/8$ inch thick, thin and crisp cookies will result.

Cut out the cookies with your cutters and transfer the cookies with a metal spatula to the prepared baking sheet. Use up the dough scraps by forming them into

Witches' brew tastes even better served with a plateful of these
spooky treats, which are fun to make with little ghosts and goblins.

chocolate spiders

1 recipe Perfect Sugar Cookie dough (page 30)

$1/2$ cup unsweetened cocoa powder

1 recipe Basic Vanilla Butter Icing (page 33)

Orange food coloring

24 feet black string licorice

48 Skittles or other round fruit-flavored candy

Prepare the dough as directed but reduce the amount of flour to $2^{1/2}$ cups
and add the cocoa powder with the flour. Chill the dough for at least
1 hour. Roll out the dough and cut it into rounds using a 2- or 3-inch cookie
cutter. Bake as directed. Cool thoroughly on wire racks.

Tint the icing with the food coloring. Generously frost half the cookies,
then top each with another cookie. Cut the licorice into $1^{1/2}$-inch lengths.
Carefully insert 4 licorice "legs" into each side of the cookie. Place 2 tiny
dabs of frosting on top of each sandwich cookie, and attach 2 Skittle "eyes"
to each cookie. These are best eaten the day they are made and don't freeze
well. You can freeze the undecorated cookies in an airtight container for
up to 2 months.

MAKES 2 DOZEN SPIDERS

a ball, re-rolling them, and cutting them out. You may need to refrigerate the dough for 15 minutes or so after you've rolled it out a couple of times because it warms up, but then it should be perfectly pliable once again.

In the old days, cooks liberally greased their baking sheets without thinking twice. But actually, a lavish greasing of the pan just means that your cookies will spread out too much and thus have a tendency to burn. If a pan is to be greased, do so sparingly, or use a nonstick cooking spray that doesn't add a lot of unwanted calories. Better yet, use parchment, since it adds no fat at all and is ultra convenient. Just slide the whole piece of parchment paper off the baking sheet and you won't have to remove the cookies one by one with a spatula.

Ideally, you'd just bake one pan of cookies at a time to ensure even heat. But most of us don't have that much leisure time so we double up and bake two pans at once. For evenly baked cookies, rotate the pans from the top shelf to the bottom shelf of the oven, and from front to back, at least once during the baking process. If you are only baking one sheet or pan of cookies, place it on the middle oven shelf unless the recipe instructions specify otherwise. Preheat the oven at least 15 minutes before you put in the cookies.

If you like your cookies soft and chewy, remove them from the oven after the minimum baking time. If you prefer crisp cookies, bake longer. Remember that cookies continue to "bake" for a little while when they come out of the oven, so even cookies that appear soft and mushy will set and firm up as they cool.

CHOCOLATE BRANDY COOKIES continued

the oven, use a spatula to transfer them to a rack, and cool completely. When the cookies are cool, sandwich them together with the Coconut Filling. Store the cookies in the refrigerator, tightly wrapped for up to 2 days. These cookies do not freeze well once assembled, but you can freeze the plain cookies, in an airtight container, for up to 1 month.

MAKES 20 COOKIES

The dough for these fancy cookies should be made a couple of hours ahead and kept in the refrigerator. If you like, substitute Cream Filling (page 39) or simply raspberry jam instead.

chocolate brandy cookies with coconut filling

Two 1-ounce squares unsweetened chocolate, melted

$^{1}/_{2}$ cup (1 stick) unsalted butter, at room temperature

1 cup sugar

1 egg

1 tablespoon brandy

$1^{1}/_{2}$ teaspoons pure vanilla extract

$1^{1}/_{4}$ cups all-purpose flour plus more if needed

$^{1}/_{4}$ teaspoon salt

$1^{1}/_{2}$ teaspoons baking powder

Coconut Filling (page 38)

Melt the chocolate in a microwave oven on Medium, stirring after each 30-second increment. Set it aside to cool.

In the bowl of an electric mixer set on medium speed, beat the butter with the sugar. Beat in the egg, brandy, and vanilla. Stir in the melted, cooled chocolate.

In a sifter, combine the flour, salt, and baking powder. Sift into the butter mixture. If the dough is really sticky, beat in another couple of tablespoons flour.

Form the dough into a 2-inch diameter roll, wrap in waxed paper, and refrigerate for at least 4 hours.

Preheat the oven to 400°F. Using a sharp knife, cut the roll of dough into 40 slices. Place the cookies on ungreased baking sheet, cut side up, rotating the pans from top to bottom once, for about 8 minutes. The cookies are done when they are beginning to color on the bottom. Remove the cookies from

continued

Cookie Decorating

Decorating cookies brings out the artistic inner child in all of us, and it certainly can be the most visually gratifying part of the whole project.

If you plan to decorate often, you may want to pick up an inexpensive kit for under $15 that includes just the basics: three decorating tips with star, basket weave, and writing capabilities; some disposable 10- or 12-inch pastry bags; little jars of liquid food coloring; and a 4-inch icing spatula. Be sure to get enough pastry bags so you can have several colors of frosting ready at the same time. Either gel or paste food coloring is recommended as they produce vibrant colors with only one or two drops of color.

Once your frosting is made and you are ready to fill the pastry bag with frosting, cut about $1^1/_2$ inches off the tip of the bag, then insert a decorating tube, pushing it through the small end of the bag so that its tip is exposed. Fold the top of the bag back about an inch or so to form a cuff. Fill about three-quarters full, unfold the cuff, and twist the top. If it's hard to keep the bag steady enough to fill it, place the bag inside a heavy drinking glass and fold the top back over the rim of the cup. Spoon and scrape the icing into the bag, using a small spatula. Then remove the bag from the cup and twist the top to hold in the frosting. If you secure it with a rubber band or a twist tie, the bag will stay closed and you won't get icing all over your hands. Now you can apply pressure by hand to force the icing out. If you plan to change tip shapes, a plastic coupler placed in the bag before the tips permits you to do this without filling another whole bag.

You really only need about three tips to make gorgeous cookies. The star tip will give you perfect stars as well as a pretty border. The round small tip is handy for writing and for piping outlines, and the basket weave tip gives a nice border and a scalloped effect.

If you want a faster route to beautiful cookies, simply invest in sprinkles of every color, to be applied while the icing is still wet. If you put all the sprinkles into small cups and then work over one large baking sheet, the mess will be contained to the baking sheet and not all over the kitchen counter and floor.

PEANUT BUTTER CHOCOLATE MARBLE SQUARES continued

In a medium bowl, sift together the flour, salt, and baking powder. In the bowl of an electric mixer set on medium, beat the sugar into the chocolate mixture until smooth. Beat in the eggs, vanilla, and flour mixture.

To make the peanut butter batter:
In a medium bowl, beat the peanut butter, butter, sugar, and vanilla until smooth.

Pour half the chocolate batter into the prepared pan. Drop tablespoonfuls of the peanut butter batter onto the top, using almost all of it and leaving about 1 inch of space between the spoonfuls. Top with remaining chocolate batter and the last few spoonfuls of the peanut butter batter. Swirl the peanut butter batter by running a knife through the pan. You want to get a marbleized effect.

Bake for 35 to 40 minutes, until fairly firm. Allow to cool in the pan for 20 minutes. Lift the squares out of the pan by holding onto the parchment paper that extends from the pan and tugging gently. Cut into squares when cool. Store in a single layer, tightly wrapped, for up to 4 days in the refrigerator. To freeze, wrap tightly for up to 1 month.

MAKES 16 SQUARES

You can also do some pretty creative decorating with candy and coconut. Place some coconut in a small plastic bag with the food coloring of your choice (green works well for grass). Work the food coloring around until the coconut is a uniform shade of green, then sprinkle it on a freshly iced cookie. You can use M & M's and Skittles to be a "pizza topping" or arrange them in lines to be a caterpillar. Don't overlook chocolate chips and raisins when you need eyes and buttons for gingerbread men, or candy corn when you need an eerie grin on an orange-frosted pumpkin cookie.

Candy can be useful trim in other ways, too. Shoestring licorice becomes spider legs or hair on a monster. Colorful sugar wafer candies can double as heads or bodies of whatever you happen to be constructing on a frosted cookie. Miniature marshmallows, gummy candy, and gumdrops can be applied to whatever colorful frosting you like.

Some bakers like to brush the cookies with a glaze when they come out of the oven, before decorating them. This works especially well on softer cookies to seal in the moisture and prepare the surface for the actual frosting.

If you're planning to use jam or preserves in your decorating, make it look extra fancy by piping it out of a plastic squeeze bottle with a narrow opening in three rows over a plate of frosted brownies. Then run a knife through the stripes to form them into a decorative pattern. Try using strawberry or raspberry jam over vanilla, chocolate, or cream cheese icing. You can also achieve a marbled effect by dropping small dots of a colored or a chocolate frosting onto a cookie that you have frosted white. Drag the edges of a toothpick through the vanilla frosting, swirling it slightly, to get pretty designs.

A simple way to decorate biscotti or any plain butter cookie is to melt either white or dark chocolate and put it into a pastry bag or a zip-top sandwich bag. Snip about $1/8$ inch off the corner of the bag, and then drizzle the melted chocolate in a decorative pattern over your cookies. Use melted white or dark chocolate in a pastry bag to outline hearts, shamrocks, or stars on just about any cookie you want. When it comes to decorating cookies, the only limit is your imagination, so think sweet thoughts and let your creative side shine through!

Chocolate and peanut butter just may be the perfect combination in a cookie, and here the two flavors meet in a marbleized square that appeals to the inner child in all of us. These freeze well, too, so it pays to make two pans at a time. If you're planning any fall parties, these squares, cut very small, are pretty on a dessert buffet.

peanut butter chocolate marble squares

Butter for the baking pan

For the chocolate batter:

6 ounces semisweet chocolate, cut into small pieces (or 1 cup of semisweet chocolate chips)

$^1/_4$ cup ($^1/_2$ stick) unsalted butter, cut into small pieces

$^2/_3$ cup all-purpose flour

Pinch of salt

$^1/_2$ teaspoon baking powder

$^3/_4$ cup granulated sugar

3 eggs

1 teaspoon pure vanilla extract

For the peanut butter batter:

$^3/_4$ cup smooth peanut butter

$^1/_4$ cup ($^1/_2$ stick) unsalted butter, melted

$^1/_2$ cup confectioners' sugar

1 teaspoon pure vanilla extract

Preheat the oven to 325°F and butter a 9-inch square baking pan. Line it with parchment paper, allowing the paper to hang over the sides a little bit, and butter the parchment.

To make the chocolate batter:

Place the chocolate and butter into a microwafe-safe dish and melt in the microwave on Medium, stirring every 30 seconds. Allow to cool.

continued

The kitchen smells like Thanksgiving while these moist and spicy bars are in the oven. Easy to mix, they rely on one of my favorite time-saving ingredients: canned pumpkin. Though they're delicious plain, the cream cheese icing makes them even better.

pumpkin spice bars

Cooking spray for the pans

1 cup granulated sugar

$1/2$ cup packed brown sugar

2 cups all-purpose flour

2 teaspoons baking powder

1 teaspoon baking soda

2 teaspoons ground cinnamon

$1/4$ teaspoon salt

$1/2$ teaspoon ground nutmeg

4 eggs, lightly beaten

One 16-ounce can pumpkin

1 cup canola oil

Cream Cheese Icing (page 34)

Preheat the oven to 350°F. Spray a 9 by 13-inch baking pan and an 8-inch square baking pan with cooking spray.

In the bowl of an electric mixer, stir together the granulated sugar, brown sugar, flour, baking powder, baking soda, cinnamon, salt, and nutmeg. Add the eggs, pumpkin, and oil and beat with the mixer set on medium speed until no traces of flour remain.

Spread evenly into the prepared pans. Bake for 25 minutes or until a toothpick inserted in the center of the bars comes out clean. Remove from the oven and cool for 2 to 3 hours. Spread with Cream Cheese Icing and cut into bars. Store in a single layer, tightly wrapped, for 2 days at room temperature or 4 days in the refrigerator. To freeze, wrap tightly and place in freezer for up to 1 month.

MAKES 4 DOZEN BARS

Storing & Mailing Cookies

KEEPING COOKIES FRESH

Make sure your cookies are completely cool before you pack them, since cookies that are put away still slightly warm end up sticking to one another or breaking. As a general rule, cookies should be stored in an airtight container. Line it with plastic wrap, carefully fill with cookies, and top with a piece of plastic wrap over the opening before you cover it. Press out as much air as possible before sealing the container. Don't mix soft cookies and crisp cookies because the crisp cookies will turn soft. Most cookies will keep for about a week at room temperature when stored in an airtight container. You may reheat crisp cookies that have softened in a 325°F degree oven for about 10 minutes to recrisp them.

Some cookies, most notably those that contain fresh fruit, milk, and eggs, need to be refrigerated. Tightly cover them first with foil or plastic wrap. Be sure not to place cookies near anything in the refrigerator that has a strong odor, such as a cut onion. Most cookies also may be frozen for up to three months. Be sure to wrap securely in freezer wrap and place them in a tin to keep them from being crushed. Label and date them so you won't forget what kinds you froze.

PACKING COOKIES TO MAIL

Whether you plan to mail a box of cookies to your aunt in honor of Mother's Day or send off a batch of holiday cookies to a friend, packing them with care means they'll arrive intact, and not as a batch of sad-looking crumbs. Rather than fragile cookies, mail sturdier items like bars and chewy drop cookies.

Line the bottom and sides of a heavy box or a large tin with plastic bubble wrap or even plain popcorn. Place the cookies in a single layer, as snugly as possible so they won't shift in transit, and cushion each layer of cookies with a layer of plastic bubble wrap. Fill the box as full as possible, then put this into a larger box and scatter some packing material in the space between the cookie box or tin and the larger box. Close the box, secure firmly with tape, mark it "Fragile," and mail as soon as possible.

pumpkin spice bars

Source Guide

If you don't live near a cookware store or gourmet supermarket, that doesn't mean you can't get the best ingredients, utensils, and bakeware needed to produce perfect cookies. Here's a list of places where you can order online or by phone.

For cookware, utensils, and baking equipment:

Baker's Catalogue
www.bakerscatalogue.com
800-827-6836

Bowery Kitchen Supplies
www.shopbowery.com
212-376-4982

Bridge Kitchenware
www.bridgekitchenware.com
212-688-4220
800-274-3435

Broadway Panhandler
www.broadwaypanhandler.com
212-966-3434
866-266-5927

Cooking.com
www.cooking.com
800-663-8810

King Arthur Flour
www.kingarthurflour.com
800-827-6836

Sur La Table
www.surlatable.com
800-243-0852

Williams-Sonoma
www.williams-sonoma.com
877-812-6235

Zabar's
www.zabars.com
800-697-6301

For ingredients like chocolate, candy, and nuts:

Chocosphere
www.chocosphere.com
877-992-4626

Economy Candy
www.economycandy.com
212-254-1531
800-352-4544

Kalustyan's
www.kalustyans.com
212-685-3451
800-352-3451

Penzey's Spices
www.penzeys.com
800-741-7787

Chock-full of fruits and nuts, these chewy bars are delicious for a snack or dessert. Wrap them individually and tote to a fall picnic or tailgate party, or nibble one in the morning with a cup of coffee.

harvest walnut date bars

$3/4$ cup walnut pieces

Butter for the baking pan

$1/2$ cup all-purpose flour

$1 1/2$ teaspoons ground cinnamon

$1/4$ teaspoon ground nutmeg

$3/4$ teaspoon baking powder

$1/8$ teaspoon salt

$2 1/2$ cups dried, pitted, chopped dates

$1/2$ cup (1 stick) unsalted butter, melted and cooled

$1/2$ cup packed dark brown sugar

2 eggs

$1 1/2$ teaspoons pure vanilla extract

Preheat the oven to 375°F. Place the walnuts in a single layer on a baking sheet and toast, stirring occasionally, for 10 minutes or until golden brown. Cool and roughly chop.

Butter a 9-inch square baking pan and line it with parchment paper, leaving about a 1-inch overhang. Butter the parchment paper.

In a large bowl, stir together the flour, cinnamon, nutmeg, baking powder, and salt. Add the dates and the walnuts and toss to combine.

In the bowl of an electric mixer set on low speed, beat the melted butter with the brown sugar, eggs, and vanilla. Stir this into the date mixture. Spread the batter evenly in the prepared pan. Bake for 25 minutes, or until the bars are golden and fairly firm in the center. Cool in the pan. Cut into bars and store in an airtight container, between layers of waxed paper, for up to 3 days or freeze for up to 1 month.

MAKES 9 BARS

Basic Cookies & Icings

These frosted, fruit-filled gems will remind you of the classic apple dessert. If you want to gild the lily, sprinkle each frosted cookie with some chopped nuts.

apple cobblers

Nonstick cooking spray

$^1/_2$ cup (1 stick) butter, softened

1 $^1/_3$ cups packed dark brown sugar

1 egg

1 teaspoon ground cloves

1 teaspoon ground cinnamon

$^1/_4$ teaspoon ground nutmeg

$^1/_2$ teaspoon salt

1 teaspoon baking soda

1 $^3/_4$ cups all-purpose flour

$^1/_4$ cup milk

$^3/_4$ cup golden raisins

1 cup chopped pecans

1 large apple, peeled and diced (about 1 cup)

1 recipe Basic Vanilla Butter Icing (page 33)

Preheat the oven to 400°F and line 2 baking sheets with parchment or spray them with nonstick cooking spray.

In the bowl of an electric mixer set on medium speed, beat the butter until light. Add the brown sugar and beat well. Beat in the egg.

Sift together the cloves, cinnamon, nutmeg, salt, baking soda, and flour. Sift this into the butter mixture in 2 parts, alternating with the milk. When the dough is well mixed, stir in the raisins, pecans, and apple by hand. Drop tablespoonfuls of the dough onto the prepared baking sheets. Bake for about 10 minutes, until the cookies are light brown on the bottom and golden on top. Remove to racks to cool. Spread the cookies with the icing when cool, and store them in an airtight container for up to 3 days or freeze for up to 1 month.

MAKES 3 DOZEN COBBLERS

perfect sugar cookies

2   sticks (1 cup) unsalted butter, at room temperature

1   cup sugar, plus more for sprinkling

2   eggs

2   teaspoons pure vanilla extract

3   cups all-purpose flour

$3/4$ teaspoon salt

$1/2$ teaspoon baking soda

In the bowl of an electric mixer set on medium speed, beat the butter until creamy and light, about 2 minutes. Gradually add the sugar and beat well. Add the eggs one at a time and beat well. Beat in the vanilla.

Sift together the flour, salt, and baking soda. Add it in 2 batches to the creamed mixture, beating for about 30 seconds each time. The dough should be firm and cohesive, but not sticky. Cover with plastic wrap and refrigerate for about 1 hour. If you plan to make several different kinds of cookies with this dough, form into several balls, wrap each in plastic, and refrigerate.

Preheat the oven to 375°F. Drop the dough, using 1 heaping teaspoon per cookie, onto ungreased baking sheets. Sprinkle with a little granulated sugar. Bake for 10 to 12 minutes, until golden. Remove to wire racks to cool completely. Store in an airtight container for up to 1 week or freeze for up to 2 months.

MAKES 5 DOZEN COOKIES

apple cobblers

This classic cookie with a crosshatch pattern across the top features a double dose of peanut flavor thanks to the addition of chopped peanuts. I prefer using salted peanuts because they enhance the nutty flavor of the cookies but you may also use unsalted peanuts.

double peanut butter cookies

$1/2$ cup (1 stick) unsalted butter, at room temperature

$1/2$ cup peanut butter (creamy or chunky)

$1/2$ cup granulated sugar

$1/2$ cup packed brown sugar

1 egg

1 teaspoon pure vanilla extract

$1 1/4$ cups all-purpose flour

$3/4$ teaspoon baking soda

$1/4$ teaspoon salt

$1/2$ cup chopped salted peanuts

Preheat the oven to 350°F. In the mixing bowl of an electric mixer set on medium speed, beat the butter for 30 seconds. Add the peanut butter and both the sugars, and beat for 2 minutes or until fluffy. Beat in the egg and the vanilla.

Sift together the flour, baking soda, and salt. Sift the flour into the butter mixture and beat for 1 minute or until well combined. Stir in the peanuts by hand.

Roll the dough into 48 balls and place them about 1 inch apart on ungreased baking sheets. Lightly press the tines of a fork into each cookie, first in one direction and then in the other, to make a crisscross pattern. The cookies should be about $1 1/2$ inches in diameter.

Bake the cookies for 10 minutes or until the edges are golden brown. Remove from the oven, transfer to a wire rack with a spatula, and cool completely. Store in an airtight container for up to 1 week or freeze for up to 2 months.

MAKES 4 DOZEN COOKIES

Old fashioned, homey cookies that are sturdy enough to pile into a cookie jar or send in a child's lunch, these are good keepers. In place of raisins, you can use dried cranberries or chopped dates.

walnut raisin jumbles

Nonstick cooking spray

1 cup (2 sticks) unsalted butter, at room temperature

1 cup granulated sugar

1 cup packed brown sugar

2 eggs

3 cups sifted all-purpose flour

1^1/$_2$ teaspoons baking soda

^{1}/$_2$ teaspoon salt

2 teaspoons pure vanilla extract

1 cup raisins

1 cup coarsely chopped walnuts

Preheat the oven to 375°F. Line 2 baking sheets with parchment paper or lightly spray them with cooking spray.

In the bowl of an electric mixer set on medium speed, beat the butter with both sugars until light and fluffy. Beat in the eggs.

Measure the flour, baking soda, and salt into a sifter. Sift it into the butter mixture and beat for 1 or 2 minutes, until well blended. Beat in the vanilla. Stir the raisins and the walnuts into the dough.

Form into balls, using about a tablespoon per cookie, and place on the prepared baking sheets. Flatten each ball slightly. Bake the cookies for 10 to 12 minutes or until lightly golden and set, rotating the pans once during the baking process. With a spatula, remove the cookies to a rack to finish cooling. Store at room temperature in an airtight container for up to 1 week or freeze for up to 3 months.

MAKES 3 DOZEN JUMBLES

Crisp, crunchy, and classic, this is an endlessly versatile recipe. Add toasted pecans, stir in shredded coconut, toss in a handful of raisins or dried cranberries—or keep them as they are, plain, simple, and good.

chocolate chip cookies

1 cup (2 sticks) unsalted butter, at room temperature

$^3/_4$ cup packed light brown sugar

$^3/_4$ cup granulated sugar

2 eggs

$1^1/_2$ teaspoons pure vanilla extract

$2^1/_2$ cups all-purpose flour

1 teaspoon salt

1 teaspoon baking soda

1 teaspoon warm water

3 cups semisweet chocolate chips

Preheat the oven to 375° F and lightly grease 2 baking sheets.

In the bowl of an electric mixer set on medium speed, beat the butter until creamy and light, about 2 minutes. Add both sugars and beat well. Add the eggs and vanilla and beat until fluffy.

Sift together the flour and salt. In a small cup, stir the baking soda into the water; set aside. Add half the flour mixture to the butter mixture and beat well. Beat in the baking soda mixture and then the remaining flour mixture. Stir in the chocolate chips by hand.

Drop the dough, using about 1 tablespoon per cookie, onto the baking sheets, spacing the cookies $1^1/_2$ inches apart. Flatten the cookies so that they measure about $1^1/_2$ inches in diameter. Bake for 10 minutes or until lightly browned and crisp. Remove the cookies from the baking sheets with a spatula and cool on wire racks. Store in an airtight container for up to 1 week or freeze for up to 2 months.

MAKES 6 DOZEN COOKIES

These crunchy-chewy cookies always disappear fast. They're great to take along on an autumn picnic or tailgate party, and are an excellent cookie for a child's lunchbox, too, as they contain nutritious rolled oats and corn flakes.

coconut oat jumbles

Butter for the baking sheets

$1^3/4$ cups all-purpose flour

1 teaspoon baking soda

$1/4$ teaspoon salt

$1^1/2$ teaspoons baking powder

1 cup (2 sticks) unsalted butter, at room temperature

1 cup granulated sugar

1 cup packed brown sugar

2 eggs

$1^1/2$ teaspoons pure vanilla extract

1 cup rolled oats (not quick-cooking oatmeal)

2 cups corn flakes, coarsely crushed

1 cup sweetened coconut flakes

Preheat the oven to 350°F. Lightly butter 2 baking sheets. Sift together the flour, baking soda, salt, and baking powder.

In the bowl of an electric mixer set on medium speed, beat the butter with both sugars until fluffy. Add the eggs and vanilla and beat well. Sift in the flour mixture and beat until combined. Stir in the oats, corn flakes, and coconut. Drop the dough onto the prepared baking sheets, using 1 rounded teaspoonful for each cookie. Bake for 9 to 12 minutes, until golden brown. Use a wide spatula to transfer the cookies to a rack to cool. Store in an airtight container for up to 3 days or freeze for up to 1 month.

MAKES 5 DOZEN JUMBLES

basic vanilla butter icing

3 cups confectioners' sugar

3 tablespoons unsalted butter, softened

1/3 cup whole milk

1 teaspoon pure vanilla extract

In the bowl of an electric mixer set on high speed beat together the sugar, butter, milk, and vanilla for 3 minutes. When icing is smooth and spreadable, you may use immediately or refrigerate. Store in an airtight container, in the refrigerator, for up to 3 days. This icing does not freeze well.

MAKES ABOUT 1 1/2 CUPS, ENOUGH TO FROST 3 DOZEN COOKIES

This may be tinted to the color of your choice.

royal icing

4 cups confectioners' sugar

4 tablespoons meringue powder

1/2 cup warm water

In the work bowl of an electric mixer, combine all ingredients and beat on medium speed for 10 minutes. If the mixture seems too stiff, add another teaspoon or two of warm water. Store in an airtight container, for up to 1 week.

MAKES ABOUT 2 1/2 CUPS

coconut oat jumbles

This lush icing is creamy and rich, making it the perfect topping for any number of bar, drop, or rolled cookies. Stir in some melted milk chocolate chips and voilà! You have a delicious milk chocolate cream cheese icing.

cream cheese icing

$^1/_2$ cup (1 stick) unsalted butter, at room temperature, plus more if needed

6 ounces cream cheese, softened

$1^1/_2$ teaspoons pure vanilla extract

$4^1/_2$ cups confectioners' sugar, plus more if needed

In the bowl of an electric mixer set on medium speed, beat together the butter, cream cheese, and vanilla until very smooth. Add $2^1/_4$ cups of the confectioners' sugar and beat well. Add the remaining $2^1/_4$ cups sugar and beat until creamy and spreadable. If too thick, add a bit more butter. If too thin, add a little more confectioners' sugar. Store in an airtight container, in the refrigerator, for up to 3 days. This icing does not freeze well.

MAKES ABOUT 3 CUPS, ENOUGH TO FROST 4 DOZEN COOKIES

CRANBERRY WALNUT RUGALACH continued

Brush each round of dough with a thin layer of raspberry jam, leaving about a $1/2$-inch border around the edge. Sprinkle with the walnut mixture. Cut each round of dough into 12 wedges. Roll up from the wide end toward the point and pinch the point to seal in the filling. Form crescents by bending the edges slightly. Place on the prepared baking sheets. Bake for 15 minutes or until golden. Cool on the baking sheets for 1 minute. Transfer to a rack to cool completely. Store in an airtight container for up to 3 days or freeze for up to 1 month.

MAKES 4 DOZEN RUGALACH

Similar to a simple vanilla icing but with a more intense flavor, this is an easy and pretty topping for chocolate, fruit-filled, or vanilla cookies.

browned butter frosting

$1/2$ cup (1 stick) unsalted butter

$4^{1}/_{2}$ cups sifted confectioners' sugar, plus more if needed

5 tablespoons heavy cream, plus more if needed

1 tablespoon vanilla extract

Melt the butter in a small skillet over low heat and continue to cook until it turns light brown, stirring once or twice. Remove from the heat and allow to cool.

In the bowl of an electric mixer set on medium speed, beat together the sugar, cream, vanilla, and melted butter until smooth and creamy. If too thick, add additional cream 1 teaspoon at a time and beat well after each addition. If too thin, beat in a little more confectioners' sugar. Store in an airtight container, in the refrigerator, for up to 3 days. This frosting does not freeze well.

MAKES 2 TO $2^{1}/_{2}$ CUPS, ENOUGH TO FROST 4 TO 5 DOZEN COOKIES

Tender little crescents filled with the flavors of fall, these are versatile because you can substitute raisins or chocolate chips for the dried cranberries. Chilling the dough for a couple of hours makes it much easier to handle.

cranberry walnut rugalach

For the dough:

- 1 cup (2 sticks) unsalted butter, at room temperature
- 8 ounces cream cheese, at room temperature
- 3 tablespoons sugar
- $^1/_4$ teaspoon salt
- 2 cups all-purpose flour, plus more for rolling

For the filling:

- $^1/_2$ cup finely chopped walnuts
- $^1/_2$ cup chopped dried cranberries
- $^1/_2$ cup packed brown sugar
- 2 teaspoons ground cinnamon
- 1 cup raspberry jam

To make the dough:

In the bowl of an electric mixer set on medium speed, beat the butter with the cream cheese and sugar until fluffy. Sift the salt with the flour. Add to the butter mixture and beat until just combined. Divide the dough into 4 balls, wrap in plastic, and refrigerate for 2 hours. (The dough may be frozen at this point for up to 3 months.)

Preheat the oven to 375°F. Remove the dough from the refrigerator and allow to sit at room temperature for 10 to 15 minutes. Line 2 baking sheets with parchment paper. Flour a work surface and a rolling pin. Roll out each ball of dough to a 14-inch circle.

To make the filling:

In a mixing bowl, combine the walnuts, cranberries, brown sugar, and cinnamon.

continued

When you plan to decorate, spread this on the cookies as soon as they come out of the oven. It gives them a nice "primer" and prepares them for a coat of icing. This is optional and not required for decorating the cookies.

basic glaze

2 cups confectioners' sugar

4 to 5 tablespoons water

In the bowl of an electric mixer set at medium speed, combine the sugar and the water. Beat very well. The glaze is ready when it is smooth and quite thin. Store in an airtight container, in the refrigerator, for up to 3 days. This glaze does not freeze well.

MAKES $^2/_3$ CUP

You've probably seen a variation of this recipe somewhere, maybe under the name of Five Layer Cookies. It's one of my children's absolute favorites and is also incredibly easy to make. Personalize yours by using whatever kind of chips you like: white chocolate, semisweet chocolate, butterscotch, even peanut butter. I've used mini chocolate chips and chocolate chunks, but I like the regular size chips best. Whichever flavor combo you go with, expect to get a lot of requests for this recipe!

magic cookie bars

$^1/_2$ cup (1 stick) butter, cut into 4 pieces

$1^1/_2$ cups graham cracker crumbs

One 14-ounce can sweetened condensed milk

1 cup sweetened coconut flakes

1 cup milk chocolate chips

1 cup butterscotch chips

Preheat the oven to 350°F. Place the butter into a 9 by 13-inch baking pan and put the pan in the oven for 5 minutes or until the butter is melted. Remove from the oven, cool 5 minutes, and sprinkle the graham cracker crumbs over the butter. With your fingers, moisten the crumbs with the butter and pat into an even layer.

Pour the sweetened condensed milk over the crumbs. Evenly scatter the coconut, chocolate chips, and butterscotch chips over the milk. Bake for 20 to 25 minutes or until golden brown around the edges. Be careful not to overbake or the cookies around the edges of the pan will be dry and hard. The middle of the pan should still be slightly jiggly when the cookies are done. Cool in the pan for about 30 minutes before cutting into bars. Store in an airtight container, between layers of waxed paper, for up to 4 days or freeze for up to 1 month.

MAKES 2 DOZEN BARS

Give cookies and biscotti a professional touch by dipping them into this glaze and then, if you like, coating them with finely chopped nuts, coconut, or sprinkles. If the glaze starts to get too thick, simply stir and cook it over very low heat for a minute.

chocolate glaze

$1/3$ cup light corn syrup

1 cup sugar

$1/3$ cup water

$1 1/2$ cups semisweet chocolate chips

$1/2$ teaspoon pure vanilla extract

In a small saucepan, combine the corn syrup, sugar, and water. Cook over low heat, stirring, until it boils. Let it boil vigorously as you stir it for 10 seconds. Remove the saucepan from the heat and stir in the chocolate chips. Allow to stand for 3 minutes, then whisk in the vanilla and continue to stir until smooth. Store in an airtight container, in the refrigerator, for up to 3 days. This glaze does not freeze well.

MAKES 1 $1/2$ CUPS

magic cookie bars

This filling is especially nice with all kinds of chocolate cookies.

It's a terrific foil for vanilla shortbread cookies, too.

coconut filling

1 egg

$^1/_2$ cup packed brown sugar

4 teaspoons all-purpose flour

$1^1/_2$ cups sweetened coconut flakes

$^1/_2$ teaspoon pure vanilla extract

In a saucepan, beat the egg. Add the brown sugar, flour, and coconut. Cook over low heat until it boils, stirring. Remove from heat, stir in the vanilla and allow to cool thoroughly before using. Store in an airtight container, in the refrigerator, for up to 2 days. This filling does not freeze well.

MAKES $1^1/_2$ CUPS

Fall

Summer

Enjoy this variation on the classic Toll House cookie with a glass of minted iced tea and you'll feel cool all over.

double mint chocolate chip cookies

1 recipe Chocolate Chip Cookie dough (page 32) made with 2 cups mint chocolate chips

1 tablespoon very finely chopped fresh mint

Chocolate Glaze (page 37, optional)

Preheat the oven to 375°F. Line 2 baking sheets with parchment paper.

Prepare the dough, adding the chopped mint with the eggs. Drop the dough by tablespoonfuls onto the prepared baking sheets.

Bake for 10 minutes or until golden brown. Remove the cookies from the oven and allow to stand for 1 minute. With a spatula, remove the cookies to a wire rack to finish cooling. If you like, drizzle with Chocolate Glaze when cool. When the cookies are completely cool, store in an airtight container for up to 3 days or freeze for up to 1 month.

MAKES 3 DOZEN COOKIES

chocolate chip ice cream sandwich cookies

after the first 8 minutes. The biscotti are done when they are crisp and light brown. With a spatula, transfer them to a wire rack and allow to cool.

Dip 1 end of each cookie into the Chocolate Glaze and set on waxed paper until the glaze dries. Store in an airtight container, between layers of waxed paper, for up to 3 days or freeze for up to 1 month.

MAKES 3 DOZEN BISCOTTI

Make these ahead of time, wrap and freeze individually, and then bring out at the end of a barbecue or outdoor birthday party for a special dessert.

chocolate chip ice cream sandwich cookies

1 recipe Chocolate Chip Cookie dough (page 32)

1 quart premium ice cream, slightly softened

One 12 ounce bag (2 cups) mini chocolate chips

Bake the cookies according to directions and allow them to cool thoroughly on wire racks. Arrange 3 dozen of the cookies, flat side up, on a work surface. Spread each with some ice cream. Top with another cookie, making sure the flat side is facing the ice cream. Roll the ice cream edge of each sandwich in chocolate chips so that the ice cream layer is coated in chips. Wrap each in plastic wrap and freeze for up to 2 months. Remove from the freezer about 10 minutes before you plan to serve them.

MAKES 3 DOZEN SANDWICH COOKIES

Crunchy and very traditional Italian cookies, these almond-flavored gems are delicious with a cup of espresso.

chocolate-dipped almond biscotti

1 cup whole almonds

2 cups all-purpose flour

1 teaspoon baking powder

$1/4$ teaspoon salt

1 cup sugar

$1/4$ cup ($1/2$ stick) unsalted butter, at room temperature

2 eggs

1 teaspoon pure vanilla extract

1 recipe Chocolate Glaze (page 37)

Preheat the oven to 350°F. Line a baking sheet with parchment paper. Place the almonds in a single layer on the baking sheet and toast for 10 minutes, stirring twice, until nicely browned. Cool and chop coarsely in a food processor fitted with the steel blade.

Sift together the flour, baking powder, and salt. In the bowl of an electric mixer set on medium speed, beat the sugar and butter for several minutes, until fluffy. Beat in the eggs and the vanilla. Sift in the flour mixture and beat until just combined. Stir in the chopped almonds.

Divide the dough in half and form each half into a 12 by 2-inch loaf. Place on the baking sheet. Press down lightly to flatten.

Bake for 30 minutes or until the loaves are golden brown. Remove the loaves from the oven, turn the oven heat down to 325°F, and use a spatula to transfer the loaves to a rack to cool.

Slice each cooled loaf on the diagonal into individual biscotti. You should get about 18 cookies from each loaf. Arrange the slices in a single layer on the baking sheet, cut side down, and bake for 10 to 15 minutes, flipping

continued

The classic campfire confection with a twist: the graham crackers are homemade. To serve to kids, use milk chocolate squares, of course, but consider turning this into a slightly sophisticated sweet by using dark chocolate for grownups!

super s'mores

For the graham crackers:

1 egg

$^{1}/_{4}$ cup ($^{1}/_{2}$ stick) unsalted butter, at room temperature

$^{1}/_{3}$ cup sugar

$^{1}/_{4}$ cup honey

$^{1}/_{2}$ teaspoon baking soda

2 teaspoons water

$^{1}/_{2}$ teaspoon salt

$1^{1}/_{2}$ cups graham flour, plus more for dusting

$^{3}/_{4}$ cup all-purpose flour

For the s'mores:

16 large marshmallows

16 squares milk or dark chocolate (two 5-ounce bars)

Preheat the oven to 350°F and have ready 2 baking sheets.

To make the graham crackers:
In the bowl of an electric mixer set on medium speed, beat the egg. Add the butter, sugar, and honey and beat until creamy.

In a small cup, dissolve the baking soda in the water. Stir it into the butter mixture. Add the salt and both flours and stir to blend. The dough should hold together and not be overly dry. If it is add a little bit more water, just a teaspoon at a time.

continued

CHOCOLATE-GLAZED MILK CHOCOLATE BARS continued

In a large mixing bowl, whisk the sugar, vanilla, salt, and eggs. Add the flour and stir well. Add the cooled chocolate mixture to the flour mixture and stir to combine. Scrape and spoon the batter into the prepared baking pan. Bake for 30 minutes or until a toothpick inserted into the pan comes out clean. Cool the cookies in the pan.

To make the glaze:
In a small saucepan over low heat, cook the chocolate chips, corn syrup, and butter until well blended and melted. Remove from the heat, stir in the vanilla, and cool for 5 minutes. Spread the glaze evenly over the top of the pan and cut into 24 cookies. Store in an airtight container, between layers of waxed paper, for up to 3 days or freeze for up to 1 month.

MAKES 2 DOZEN BARS

SUPER S'MORES continued

Dust a work surface with a little graham flour and roll out the dough to a ¼-inch thickness. Cut the dough into 4 large pieces, then score the dough with a sharp knife into 2-inch squares. Don't cut all the way through. Prick each square with fork tines in several places. Place the dough onto the cookie sheets, using a wide spatula. Bake for 7 minutes, flip and bake for 6 minutes more. Cool the graham cracker squares on wire racks. Break them into individual graham crackers.

To make the s'mores:
Toast a marshmallow over a campfire or over the flame on the stove. If you don't have a gas stove or grill you could also use a small Sterno stove or microwave oven. When the marshmallow is as toasted as you like, place it on a graham cracker along with a chocolate square. Top with another graham cracker square and eat immediately.

MAKES ABOUT 16 S'MORES

The seven-ounce bar of milk chocolate needed to make these rich confections is a handy size to keep for preparing S'mores (page 64), so you may want to pick up a couple of them. You can use any brand that you like: for this cookie, I'm partial to Hershey's. Be sure to use butter, not margarine, because it really brings out the flavor of milk chocolate. You can cut these very tiny if you wish, though chocoholics would probably prefer an oversized version.

chocolate-glazed milk chocolate bars

For the batter:

$3/4$ cup ($1 1/2$ sticks) unsalted butter, cut into chunks

One 7-ounce bar milk chocolate, broken into pieces

$1/2$ cup semisweet chocolate chips

$1 1/2$ cups sugar

$1 1/2$ teaspoons pure vanilla extract

$1/4$ teaspoon salt

5 eggs

$1 1/4$ cups all-purpose flour

For the glaze:

1 cup milk chocolate chips

1 tablespoon light corn syrup

3 tablespoons unsalted butter

$1 1/2$ teaspoons pure vanilla extract

Preheat the oven to 350°F. Butter a 9 by 13-inch baking pan.

To make the batter:
In a heavy saucepan over low heat, cook the butter, milk chocolate, and semisweet chocolate chips until melted, stirring. Allow to cool.

continued

You'll find a version of these all over New York City, where they're wrapped individually and measure about the size of a small plate— definitely enough sugar to satisfy a serious sweet tooth. This recipe makes jumbo cookies but you can also bake them smaller, in which case you should reduce the oven time by at least 5 minutes. In the interests of those who don't like frosting or wish to keep their sugar intake down, it's thoughtful to leave a few of these uniced. Wrap these individually and carry along to an alfresco feast!

classic black & white cookies

For the cookies:

$3/4$ cup ($1 1/2$ sticks) unsalted butter, at room temperature

1 cup granulated sugar

2 eggs

1 teaspoon pure vanilla extract

$2 1/2$ cups all-purpose flour

$1/2$ teaspoon salt

1 teaspoon baking soda

$2/3$ cup plain yogurt

For the icing:

4 cups confectioners' sugar

3 tablespoons light corn syrup

$1/2$ teaspoon pure vanilla extract

2 tablespoons unsweetened cocoa powder

To make the cookies:
Preheat the oven to 350°F. Line 2 baking sheets with parchment paper.
In the bowl of an electric mixer set on medium speed, beat the butter with the granulated sugar until fluffy. Beat in the eggs and the vanilla.
Sift together the flour, salt, and baking soda. Add it to the butter mixture alternately with the yogurt, beating after each addition.

continued

chocolate glazed milk chocolate bars

Using about 2 generous tablespoons of dough per cookie, roll the dough into balls and place them on the baking sheet about 2 inches apart. Bake for at least 15 minutes or until golden brown, rotating the pans from top to bottom and back to front once or twice during the baking time. Remove the cookies to wire racks and allow to cool completely.

To make the icing:
In the bowl of an electric mixer set on medium speed, beat the confectioners' sugar, corn syrup, and vanilla together. Add 4 tablespoons of water and beat again. Add more water, 1 tablespoon at a time, until the frosting is of spreadable consistency. If it gets too runny, add a little more confectioners' sugar. Divide the icing between 2 bowls. Add the cocoa powder to 1 bowl and mix well.

Ice the flat side of each cookie, using vanilla icing on 1 side and chocolate icing on the other. Allow the cookies to stay on the racks until the icing is thoroughly dried. Wrap individually in plastic for up to 3 days or freeze for up to 1 month.

MAKES 1 $^1/_2$ DOZEN GIANT COOKIES

Buttery rich cookies that are both crisp and tender, these are good keepers. In fact, they taste even better after a couple of days! Traditionally, shortbread was baked in a round shape and cut into wedges. I prefer to pat the dough out into a large rectangle and cut it into fingers. To gild the lily, dip one end of each cookie into melted white chocolate and then into rainbow jimmies.

vanilla shortbread fingers

1½ cups (3 sticks) unsalted butter,
at room temperature

1 cup sugar

1 teaspoon pure vanilla extract

4 cups all-purpose flour,
plus more for kneading

Preheat the oven to 300°F. In the bowl of an electric mixer set on medium speed, beat the butter for 3 minutes. When it is pale and very creamy, add the sugar in a thin stream, beating constantly. Beat in the vanilla.

Sift the flour and then measure out 4 cups. Add the flour to the butter mixture and beat until it is well combined. The mixture should be crumbly but not overly sticky. Turn it out onto a floured work surface and knead it with the heel of your hand until it sticks together. Divide into 2 pieces. Place 1 piece onto a large ungreased baking sheet and press and pat it into a large rectangle that is about ½-inch thick. Trim away the edges with a sharp knife. Cut the dough into 4-inch strips that are each about ¾-inch wide. Prick the surface of each cookie with the tines of a fork in several places. Repeat with the remaining piece of dough and another ungreased baking sheet.

Bake the cookies for 30 to 35 minutes until very pale golden, rotating the sheets once. Cool for 5 minutes on the baking sheet. With a sharp knife, cut through the cookies to completely separate them. With a spatula, remove the cookies to a wire rack to cool completely. Store in an airtight container, between layers of waxed paper, for up to 4 days or freeze for up to 2 months.

MAKES 4 DOZEN COOKIES

lemon bars

50¢

Classic, chewy cookies that are hard to resist,
these are easy to make in the food processor.

almond macaroons

  1 pound blanched almonds

1 1/4 cups sugar

  3 egg whites

 1/2 teaspoon almond extract

 1/2 teaspoon pure vanilla extract

     Whole blanched almonds for garnish (optional)

Preheat the oven to 325°F. Line 2 baking sheets with parchment paper.

In a food processor, grind the 1 pound of almonds. Measure the almonds:
you need about 3 cups. If you don't have 3 cups after grinding the
almonds, process another cup of almonds in the food processor and add
to the ground almond mixture. Combine the sugar and the almonds in the
food processor and process until the almonds are very finely ground.
Remove to a large bowl. Add the egg whites, almond extract, and vanilla.
Mix well with your hands.

Form cookies on the prepared baking sheets, using a heaping teaspoon
for each one and leaving about 1 1/2 inches of space between each cookie.
If desired, place 1 whole blanched almond in the center of each macaroon.
Bake for 10 minutes or until golden brown. Cool for 2 minutes on the
baking sheets. Remove to a rack to finish cooling. Store in an airtight
container for up to 3 days or freeze for up to 2 months.

MAKES 3 1/2 DOZEN MACAROONS

The filling in these is pleasantly tart and the crust tastes like shortbread—delicious! If you don't serve these right away, sprinkle them with extra confectioners' sugar for a snow-white topping.

lemon bars

Butter for the baking pan

For the crust:

14 tablespoons (1 3/4 sticks) unsalted butter, chilled

1 cup sifted confectioners' sugar

1 3/4 cups all-purpose flour

1/4 teaspoon salt

For the filling:

4 or 5 large lemons

4 eggs

1 1/3 cups granulated sugar

3 tablespoons all-purpose flour

Pinch of salt

1/4 cup milk

Confectioners' sugar for dusting

Preheat the oven to 350°F and butter a 9 by 13-inch baking pan.

To make the crust:
Cut the butter into chunks and place in a food processor. Add the confectioners' sugar, flour, and salt. Process until a firm, slightly crumbly dough forms. Press into the bottom of the buttered pan. Bake for 20 minutes or until golden brown. Reduce the oven temperature to 325°F when you remove the bars from the oven.

To make the filling:
Finely grate the zest of 1 of the lemons and squeeze the juice from all the lemons. You should have about 3/4 cup of juice, and you'll need 1 teaspoon of the grated zest; set aside. In the bowl of an electric mixer, lightly beat the eggs. Beat in the granulated sugar, flour, salt, milk, and lemon zest.

continued

almond macaroons

LEMON BARS continued

Add the lemon juice and beat well.

When the crust has cooled for about 10 minutes, pour the filling over the top. Return the pan to the oven and bake for 20 to 25 minutes, until the filling is set and the bars are golden brown. When the pan has cooled, generously dust with confectioners' sugar and cut into bars. Store in the refrigerator, tightly covered in a single layer, for up to 2 days. Lemon Bars do not freeze well.

MAKES 3 DOZEN BARS

Traditional at Easter time in Greece, where they're called *kourabiedes*, these delicate butter cookies are pressed into toasted sesame seeds before baking. This dough freezes well, so make a large batch and defrost in the refrigerator for a few hours before you want to make the cookies.

sesame bow ties

$1/2$ cup sesame seeds

1 cup (2 sticks) unsalted butter, at room temperature

$1^3/4$ cups sugar

2 eggs

4 cups all-purpose flour, plus more for rolling

2 teaspoons baking powder

$1/4$ teaspoon salt

$1/4$ cup water

1 teaspoon pure vanilla extract

Preheat the oven to 350°F. Line 2 cookie sheets with parchment paper. Place the seeds on a cookie sheet and toast for 10 minutes or until golden. Remove the seeds to a small bowl and set aside. Turn off the oven.

In the bowl of an electric mixer set on medium speed, beat the butter with the sugar until fluffy. Beat in the eggs one at a time. Sift together the flour, baking powder, and salt. Add it to the butter mixture in 2 batches, alternately with the water. Beat in the vanilla. Chill the dough for 2 hours.

Preheat the oven to 350°F. Roll out the dough in several batches on a lightly floured board to about $1/4$-inch thick. Cut the dough into strips that measure about 3 by $3/4$ inch. Press each strip into the toasted sesame seeds. Fold each strip over so that it resembles a bowtie. Place on the prepared baking sheets. Bake for 10 minutes or until light golden brown. Immediately remove to a rack with a spatula and allow to cool completely. Store in an airtight container, between layers of waxed paper, for up to 3 days or freeze for up to 2 months.

MAKES 4 DOZEN BOW TIES

The taste of these creamy bars will remind you of Key Lime pie, but instead of a meringue these have a crumb topping. They'll keep well in the refrigerator for two days and are a refreshing dessert to serve in the summer. If you don't have Key limes you can use regular limes.

key lime squares

Butter for the pan

For the crust:

1 1/4 cups graham cracker crumbs

1/4 cup sugar

1/2 cup (1 stick) unsalted butter, melted and cooled

For the filling:

3 egg yolks

3 tablespoons freshly squeezed lime juice

1/2 14-ounce (1 3/4 cups) can sweetened condensed milk

Preheat the oven to 350°F. Lightly butter an 8-inch square baking dish.

To make the crust:
Stir together the graham cracker crumbs, sugar, and butter. Measure out 1/2 cup of the crumb mixture and set aside. This will be the topping. Press the remaining crumb mixture firmly into the buttered pan.

To make the filling:
In a separate bowl, beat the egg yolks until creamy. Add the lime juice and sweetened condensed milk and beat until well combined. Spoon on top of the crust and spread out evenly. Sprinkle with the crumbs. Bake for 25 to 30 minutes or until set. When cool cut into squares. Store in the refrigerator, tightly covered in a single layer, for up to 2 days. Key Lime squares do not freeze well.

MAKES 1 DOZEN SQUARES

Reminiscent of a mini pecan pie, these bite-sized cookies are irresistible. They're also versatile in that you can make them with pecans and vary the type of jam.

walnut tartlets

^{1}/$_2$ cup walnuts

1 recipe Perfect Sugar Cookie dough (page 25)

Nonstick cooking spray

2 eggs, separated

^{1}/$_2$ cup sugar

^{1}/$_8$ teaspoon salt

1 tablespoon lemon juice

^{1}/$_4$ cup apricot jam

Preheat the oven to 350°F. Chop the walnuts very fine in a food processor.

Roll out the Sugar Cookie dough to ^{1}/$_2$-inch thickness. Cut into 3-inch rounds. Press into mini muffin tins that have been sprayed with cooking spray. Flute or shape the edges with your fingers.

In the bowl of an electric mixer set to medium speed, beat the egg yolks until pale. Beat in the sugar and salt. Stir in the chopped walnuts and lemon juice. In another bowl, beat the egg whites until they form stiff peaks. Fold into the yolk mixture.

Spoon filling into each tartlet. Bake for 15 to 20 minutes, until the filling is set. Cool in the muffin tins, then remove to a rack to cool completely. Place a tiny dab of apricot jam into the center of each tartlet. Store in an airtight container at room temperature for a day or refrigerate for up to 3 days. Walnut Tartlets do not freeze well.

MAKES 3 DOZEN TARTLETS

A buttery-rich cookie with a ribbon of jam in the center, this is a good keeper and a favorite with kids. A plateful of these and a big pot of tea make a perfect midafternoon snack. Don't use jelly in place of jam because it's too runny.

strawberry jam strips

2 cups all-purpose flour, plus more for rolling

$1/2$ teaspoon baking powder

$1/4$ teaspoon salt

$3/4$ cup ($1 1/2$ sticks) unsalted butter, at room temperature

1 cup sugar

1 egg

1 teaspoon pure vanilla extract

$1/4$ cup strawberry jam (preferably not the seedless kind)

Preheat the oven to 350°F. Measure the flour, baking powder, and salt into a sifter.

In the bowl of an electric mixer set on medium speed, beat the butter with $2/3$ cup of the sugar for about 2 minutes, scraping down the bowl occasionally. Beat in the egg and the vanilla extract. Sift in the flour mixture in 3 parts, beating at low speed after each addition.

Divide the dough into 4 balls. Flour a work surface and your hands. Roll out each ball into a 12- to 14-inch log. Place the logs 3 inches apart on an ungreased baking sheet and pat out so that they are about $1 1/2$ inches wide. Press an indentation down the center of the strip, using your fingers. Be sure the indentation does not go all the way through the strip.

Use a small spoon to fill the indentation with jam. Sprinkle the top of each strip with some of the remaining $1/3$ cup sugar.

Bake for 15 to 20 minutes, until the strips are a light golden brown.

continued

72

Spray a 9 by 13-inch baking pan with cooking spray. Line it with foil, allowing the foil to hang over each end of the pan, and spray the foil with cooking spray.

Press the dough evenly into the pan and refrigerate the pan for 15 minutes.

Preheat the oven to 375°F. Bake the crust for about 25 minutes or until golden, rotating the pan once halfway through the baking time. Remove from the oven but leave the oven on.

To make the topping:
Place the pecans on a baking sheet in a single layer and toast in the oven alongside the crust for 5 to 8 minutes, until golden. When cool, chop in a food processor or by hand.

Measure the sugar into a heavy 3-quart saucepan and turn the heat to medium. When it starts to melt and turn golden, stir it occasionally. Continue to cook, stirring, and the sugar will completely melt and turn light brown. Carefully add the cream and don't worry when the mixture steams up! Stir well and cook for 30 seconds or until the mixture is smooth and liquid.

Cut the butter into little pieces. Add it to the caramel mixture along with the vanilla and salt. Stir in the chopped pecans. Pour the mixture over the partially cooled crust. Bake for 20 minutes. When it is bubbly but still jiggly, remove from the oven and cool in pan on wire rack for 2 hours. Flip the entire pan over onto a large cutting board to remove the cookies from the pan. Peel off the foil and turn right side up. Using a sharp knife, cut into 24 bars. Cut each bar in half on the diagonal. Store in an airtight container at room temperature, between layers of waxed paper for up to 1 week, or freeze for up to 3 months.

MAKES 4 DOZEN TRIANGLES

STRAWBERRY JAM STRIPS continued

Use a wide spatula to transfer the strips to a rack. After they cool for 15 minutes, move them to a work surface and cut each strip on the diagonal into 12 slices. Allow the cookies to cool completely before storing them, between layers of waxed paper, in an airtight container for up to 3 days or freezing for up to 1 month.

MAKES 4 DOZEN STRIPS

 This cookie tastes like pecan pie but is better because the ratio of pecans to filling is much higher and the crust is reminiscent of shortbread. If you've never seen sugar melt, it's fascinating to watch the solid white mound gradually melt into a caramel-colored liquid. Cut into small diamonds, these cookies make a pretty dessert on a buffet, but they are also sturdy enough to pack and mail as a gift.

pecan triangles

For the crust:

- 2 cups plus 2 tablespoons all-purpose flour
- $1/2$ teaspoon baking powder
- $1/2$ teaspoon salt
- $3/4$ cup ($1^1/2$ sticks) unsalted butter, at room temperature
- 1 cup sugar
- 1 egg
- 1 teaspoon pure vanilla extract
  Nonstick cooking spray

For the topping:

- 2 cups pecans
- $1^1/2$ cups sugar
- 1 cup heavy cream
- 6 tablespoons ($3/4$ stick) unsalted butter
- $1^1/2$ teaspoons pure vanilla extract
- $1/4$ teaspoon salt

To make the crust:
Measure the flour, baking powder, and salt into a sifter.

In the bowl of an electric mixer set on medium speed, beat together the butter and sugar for 4 minutes. Add the egg and the vanilla and beat well. Sift the flour over the creamed mixture and beat for a minute, or just until combined.

continued

When fresh blueberries are in season, try these luscious bar cookies, which have a crunchy base, lemony filling, and streusel topping. You can vary the type and proportions of berries in this cookie to suit your taste, as long as the total amount is 2 cups.

double berry streusel bites

For the streusel:

3 cups all-purpose flour

1 1/2 cups packed light brown sugar

1/2 teaspoon salt

1 teaspoon ground cinnamon

1 1/2 cups (3 sticks) unsalted butter, melted

For the filling:

1 (14-ounce) can sweetened condensed milk

1/2 cup freshly squeezed lemon juice (about 2 large lemons)

1 egg

1 egg yolk

2 tablespoons all-purpose flour

1 tablespoon grated lemon zest

1 1/2 cups blueberries

1/2 cup raspberries

Preheat the oven to 350°F. Lightly butter a 9 by 13-inch baking pan. Line with parchment paper and butter the parchment.

To make the streusel:
In a large bowl, stir together the flour, brown sugar, salt, and cinnamon. Pour in the melted butter and mix well. The mixture will be crumbly but not too dry. Press half the streusel on the bottom and an inch up the sides of the prepared baking pan. Bake for 10 minutes.

continued

pecan triangles

DOUBLE BERRY STREUSEL BITES continued

To make the filling:

In a mixing bowl, beat together the condensed milk, lemon juice, egg, egg yolk, flour, and lemon zest. Carefully stir in the berries. Spread the filling over the crust and evenly crumble the remaining streusel over the filling. Bake for 40 minutes more, until the custard is set and the streusel is crisp. Cool to room temperature, then cut into bars. Store in the refrigerator, tightly covered in a single layer, for up to 2 days. Double Berry Streusel Bites do not freeze well.

MAKES 3 DOZEN BITES

Cheerful caterpillars rest on bright green "grass" that tops a crunchy sugar cookie. These colorful cookies are perfect for a birth-day party or other outdoor gathering. If you don't have decorating bags, simply buy a couple of those teensy tubes of decorating icing in the baking section of the supermarket. Pipe smiles and eyes on the candy wafer faces. Store these cookies in a single layer on a plate until serving time.

spring caterpillars

1	recipe Perfect Sugar Cookie dough (page 30)
1	recipe Basic Vanilla Butter Icing (page 33)
	Red, black, and green food coloring
2 to 3	small bags chocolate-coated candies (such as M & M's)
2	rolls round candy wafers (such as Necco)

Bake the cookies as directed, using a 4-inch round cookie cutter. Cool completely on wire racks.

Meanwhile, tint $3/4$ of the icing bright green. Tint the remaining icing half red for the mouths and half black for the eyes. Put the red and black icings into 2 separate pastry bags outfitted with the small writing tip.

Frost each cookie with a thick coating of green icing. Beginning at the lower edge of each cookie, arrange 2 rows of chocolate coated candies so that they overlap. This is the caterpillar's body. Stick on a candy wafer for the caterpillar's head, and pipe icing to make tiny black eyes and a red smile. Store between layers of waxed paper in an airtight container for up to 3 days, or freeze for up to 1 month.

MAKES 3 DOZEN CATERPILLARS

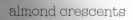
almond crescents

Indulge your inner artist when you decorate these pretty butter cookies by mixing and matching a variety of pastel shades for the icing. Once they're frosted, shake on whatever pastel-colored sprinkles you happen to have on hand. Investing in a fluted round cookie cutter will ensure even shapes for your cookies. Serve at a bridal or baby shower, or with strawberry ice cream for a festive spring dessert.

flower cutouts

1   recipe Perfect Sugar Cookie dough (page 30)
1   recipe Basic Vanilla Butter Icing (page 33) or Royal Icing (page 33)
    Pastel food coloring pastes
    Sprinkles of your choice

Preheat the oven to 375°F and line 2 baking sheets with parchment paper. Prepare the dough and chill for half an hour. Remove from the refrigerator and roll it out to a $1/4$-inch thickness. Cut out cookies with a fluted round 3- or 4-inch cookie cutter, place at least $1 1/2$ inches apart on the baking sheet, and bake for 8 to 10 minutes, depending upon the size. The cookies are done when they are golden brown. Remove from the baking sheets with a spatula and allow to cool.

Divide the Basic Vanilla Butter Icing or Royal Icing in half and tint half the icing pink and half the icing yellow. Frost each cookie with icing and top with sprinkles. Allow to dry. Store between layers of waxed paper in an airtight container for 1 week, or freeze for up to 2 months.

MAKES $3 1/2$ TO 4 DOZEN CUTOUTS

Crumbly and rich, this is a fine cookie to serve with ice cream at a summer party. You can roll and shape the cookies as large or small as you like as long as you adjust the baking time.

almond crescents

1 recipe Perfect Sugar Cookie Dough (page 30)

$1/4$ teaspoon almond extract

2 cups finely ground blanched almonds

$1 1/2$ cups sifted confectioners' sugar

Preheat the oven to 350°F. Line 2 baking sheets with parchment paper. Prepare the Sugar Cookie dough, adding the almond extract with the vanilla, and stirring in the ground almonds with the flour mixture. Break off small pieces of the dough, using about 1 tablespoon per cookie. Roll each into a $1/2$-inch length and twist it into a crescent.

Place the cookies about 1 inch apart on the baking sheets. Bake for 8 to 12 minutes until they are just beginning to color and are golden brown on the bottom. Cool completely on a wire rack.

Place the confectioners' sugar into a brown bag or plastic bag, gently add the cookies about a dozen at a time, and roll them until they are coated with sugar. Store in an airtight container for up to 3 days or freeze for up to 2 months.

MAKES 5 DOZEN CRESCENTS

With a thick coating of pleasantly tart frosting, these tender bites are fancy enough to arrange on a dessert buffet or simply to serve to friends with a pot of tea.

iced lemon snowdrops

1 recipe Perfect Sugar Cookie dough (page 30)

2 cups confectioners' sugar plus more as needed

$^1/_4$ to $^1/_3$ cup freshly squeezed lemon juice (about 2 lemons)

Chill the cookie dough for at least 2 hours.

Preheat the oven to 375°F. Line 2 baking sheets with parchment paper.

Roll the dough into 1-inch balls and place on the prepared baking sheets. Bake for 8 to 10 minutes, until the bottoms of the cookies are golden. Remove from the baking sheets and cool on a rack.

To make the glaze, beat the confectioners' sugar with $^1/_4$ cup of the lemon juice until very smooth. It should be slightly thinner than cake icing. If the glaze seems too thin, add a little bit more confectioners' sugar. If it is too thick, add more lemon juice. Dip the top of each cookie into the glaze and return the cookies to the wire rack. Wait 30 minutes, then dip the cookies into the glaze again. Let the cookies sit for an hour. When thoroughly dry, store in an airtight container, between layers of waxed paper, for up to 3 days or freeze for up to 2 months.

MAKES 5 DOZEN SNOWDROPS

Light and airy, with the crunchy goodness of pecans, these addictive little puffs melt in your mouth. In the summer, they're delicious with a large bowl of chocolate ice cream or on their own. They look pretty on a dessert buffet, and taste great a day or so after baking, too, if they last that long.

pecan meringues

3 egg whites

$^{1}/_{8}$ teaspoon salt

$^{1}/_{2}$ teaspoon cream of tartar

1 cup sugar

$1^{1}/_{2}$ cups finely chopped pecans

Preheat the oven to 200°F and line 2 baking sheets with parchment paper.

In the bowl of an electric mixer set on medium speed, beat the egg whites until foamy. Add the salt, cream of tartar, and sugar gradually. When stiff peaks form, fold in the nuts with a large spatula.

Use a teaspoon to drop spoonfuls of batter onto the prepared baking sheets. Or if you like, use a pastry bag to pipe cookies onto the baking sheets. These cookies don't spread much during the baking process so you don't have to worry about spacing them out!

Bake the cookies for 1 hour to 1 hour and 15 minutes, until crisp and barely colored on the bottom. Rotate the pans once during the baking. Remove the cookies from the oven and cool completely before storing in an airtight container for up to 3 days or freeze for up to 1 month.

MAKES 2 DOZEN MERINGUES

Classic madeleines are soft inside and crisp out. These ones are lighter than most and have a fine citrus flavor. You'll need a special madeleine pan to make these.

lemon madeleines

Butter for the molds

1 lemon¹/₂

¹/₂ cup whole almonds with skins

¹/₂ cup (1 stick) unsalted butter

4 eggs

²/₃ cup granulated sugar

¹/₂ teaspoon almond extract

1 cup all-purpose flour

Confectioners' sugar for dusting

Preheat the oven to 375°F. Lightly butter 24 madeleine molds. Finely grate the lemon. Measure out 1¹/₂ teaspoons of the lemon zest and ¹/₄ teaspoon of the lemon juice; set aside.

Toast the almonds on a baking sheet in the oven, stirring a couple of times, until they are golden brown, 6 to 8 minutes. Remove from the oven and allow to cool.

In a small saucepan, melt the butter and set it aside to cool. Grind almonds in a food processor. In the bowl of an electric mixer set on medium speed, beat the eggs with the granulated sugar for 5 minutes or until thick and pale. Add the almond extract, lemon zest, and lemon juice. Sift the flour over the egg mixture in 3 batches, stirring after each addition. Add the ground almonds and the butter and beat briefly. Spoon the batter into the prepared molds.

Bake on the lower oven rack for 10 minutes, until the edges of the cookies are golden. Remove the cookies from the oven and immediately turn them out onto a rack to cool. When they are cool, sift confectioners' sugar over the tops. Store in an airtight container, between layers of waxed paper, for up to 3 days or freeze for up to 2 months.

MAKES 2 DOZEN MADELEINES

pignoli cookies

This is a cookie you'll make over and over because it's beautiful, easy, and delicious. To avoid overbaking, take these out of the oven when they're just set. The jam should still jiggle a little when you shake the pan. If you like apricot flavor, try making these with apricot jam instead.

raspberry crumb bars

Nonstick cooking spray	$^3/_4$ teaspoon salt
$^3/_4$ cup ($1^1/_2$ sticks) unsalted butter, at room temperature	$^1/_2$ teaspoon baking soda
1 cup packed brown sugar	$1^1/_2$ cups quick-cooking oatmeal (uncooked)
$1^2/_3$ cups all-purpose flour	$1^1/_2$ cups seedless raspberry jam

Preheat the oven to 400°F and lightly spray a 9 by 13-inch baking pan with cooking spray.

In the bowl of an electric mixer set on medium speed, beat the butter for 2 minutes until it is soft and pale yellow. Beat in the brown sugar gradually.

Measure the flour, salt, and baking soda into a sifter, and sift it into the butter mixture. Beat for a minute. Beat or stir in the oats. Measure out 1 cup of the dough and set aside. Carefully press the rest of the dough into the pan, pushing with your fingers to flatten it out to the edges of the pan. Spread the jam evenly over the crust, leaving a $^1/_4$-inch margin around the edges. Evenly scatter the reserved dough over the jam.

Bake for 20 to 25 minutes, just until the crust is light brown. Cool the cookies in the pan set on a wire rack. When they are cool, cut off and discard about $^1/_2$ inch from each side of the pan. Cut the rest of the pan into 24 bars. Store for up to 3 days in an airtight container or freeze for up to 1 month.

MAKES 2 DOZEN BARS

These pretty cookies taste like almond macaroons with a generous coating of pignoli, or pine nuts. They're incredibly simple to bake and disappear quickly. For a light, pretty dessert in the summer, serve these with a bowl of fresh berries.

pignoli cookies

One 8-ounce can almond paste

1/2 cup sugar

1 egg white

Pinch of salt

1/3 cup pignoli (pine nuts)

Preheat the oven to 350°F. Line 2 baking sheets with parchment paper.

Place the almond paste, sugar, egg white, and salt into the work bowl of a food processor. Process until it is well mixed and has the consistency of a thick paste.

Put the pignoli into a shallow bowl. Using a teaspoon, drop a small amount of dough into the pignoli. Roll the cookie around to coat it with pignoli. Remove the cookie from the pignoli and form it into a small ball. Place on the prepared baking sheet. Repeat with the remaining dough until you have 2 pans of cookies. Bake for 8 to 12 minutes, depending upon the size of the cookies. Rotate the pans at least once during the baking. The cookies are done when ever so slightly golden on the top. Don't overbake these—you want them to be chewy on the inside and they'll firm up after you take them out of the oven. Store in an airtight container for up to 2 days or freeze for up to 1 month.

MAKES 2 DOZEN COOKIES

raspberry crumb bars

These are bursting with good-for-you ingredients like carrots, raisins, and wheat germ, and they taste a little bit like carrot cake. A couple of these and a glass of milk is often all my teenaged daughter wants to eat in the morning, and I figure it's better than eating no breakfast at all as she heads off to summer camp! They're as golden and warm as the summer sun and a delicious way to start the day.

morning glories

Butter for the baking sheet

For the cookies:

$^3/_4$ cup packed brown sugar

$^1/_3$ cup butter, at room temperature

1 egg

$1^1/_2$ teaspoons pure vanilla extract

$1^1/_2$ cups shredded carrot

$1^1/_4$ cups all-purpose flour

$^1/_4$ cup wheat germ

$^1/_2$ teaspoon baking soda

$^1/_2$ teaspoon salt

1 teaspoon ground cinnamon

2 cups granola with raisins

For the glaze:

$1^1/_2$ cups confectioners' sugar

3 to 4 tablespoons milk or more as needed

To make the cookies:

Preheat the oven to 350°F and lightly butter 2 baking sheets. In the bowl of an electric mixer set on medium speed, beat the brown sugar and butter until light and creamy. Beat in the egg and the vanilla. Beat in the shredded carrot until well combined.

continued

Spring

Sift together the flour, wheat germ, baking soda, salt, and cinnamon. Sift this into the butter mixture and beat until no streaks of flour are visible. Stir in the granola. Drop the batter from a teaspoon onto the prepared baking sheets, spacing the cookies about $1\frac{1}{2}$ inches apart.

Bake for 10 to 12 minutes, until slightly golden. Check the underside of the cookies and remove them from the oven when they are light brown. Cool while you make the glaze.

To make the glaze:
In a small bowl, beat the confectioners' sugar with 3 tablespoons of the milk, adding a little more milk as needed to make a slightly runny glaze. Drizzle the glaze over the cookies when they are cool. Store in an airtight container with waxed paper between the layers for up to 3 days or freeze for up to 2 months.

MAKES 3 DOZEN COOKIES

This is a good and easy-to-make filling for chocolate, lemon, or oatmeal cookies. Sandwich together a couple of cookies, then drizzle the tops with chocolate and you'll see how effortless it is to dress up a plain cookie.

cream filling

2   cups confectioners' sugar

$^1/_2$ cup (1 stick) unsalted butter, at room temperature

1   tablespoon pure vanilla extract

2   tablespoons whole milk

In the bowl of an electric mixer set on high speed, beat together the sugar, butter, vanilla, and milk until smooth and creamy. Store in an airtight container, in the refrigerator, for up to 3 days. This filling does not freeze well.

MAKES 1 CUP